Bute County
North Carolina

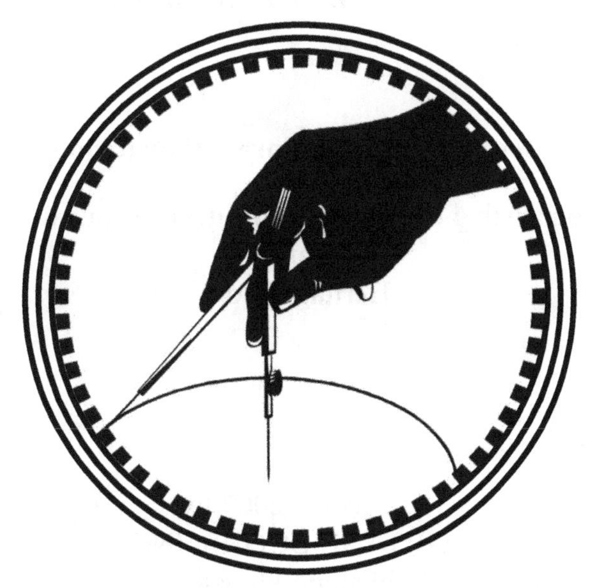

Land Grant Plats and Land Entries

COMPILED AND ABSTRACTED BY
Brent H. Holcomb

HERITAGE BOOKS
2007

HERITAGE BOOKS
AN IMPRINT OF HERITAGE BOOKS, INC.

Books, CDs, and more—Worldwide

For our listing of thousands of titles see our website
at
www.HeritageBooks.com

Published 2007 by
HERITAGE BOOKS, INC.
Publishing Division
65 East Main Street
Westminster, Maryland 21157-5026

International Standard Book Number: 978-0-7884-1689-7

Bute County was formed in 1764 from Granville County and abolished in 1779 to from Warren and Franklin Counties. There were 103 land grants issued in Bute County and one tract entered and plat made but no grant issued for it. Plats are extant for all grants, and warrants are extant for all grants except for File #12. All plats are reproduced here. Some of the originals are quite dim and faded; the copies reproduced here are as good or better than the originals. They are in approximate numberical order.

There are 345 land entries from Bute County. All of these are abstracted here. Many entries in Bute County belong to grants issued later in Warren and Franklin Counties. The original land entry book is in the North Carolina Archives at Raleigh. There is also a copy in the Franklin County Court House in Louisburg, North Carolina. I have used the original at the Archives, as the Franklin County copy appears to be a later one and contains several errors and at least one omission. There existed four documents for each land grant in this order: entry, warrant, plat, grant. Some of the plats were made on mere scraps of paper; others cover a whole page.

The index covers all surnames in the plats and land entries except for the surveyors John Dent, Joseph Hawkins, and William Christmas. Names are indexed by Plat number(P)(same as file number) and by Entry number (E), not page.

My interest in Bute County records stems from the fact that many Bute County families(e. g. Bobo, Beatman, Duke) moved to the part of Ninety Six District, South Carolina that later became Union County.

Brent Holcomb
Chapel Hill, North Carolina
June 1, 1974

Name	Acres	Grant #	File #	Date Issued	Book & Page		Entry #
Arendal, Thomas	640	83	85	12 Feb 1779	38	350	127
Ascue, Charles	640	68	70	12 Feb 1779	38	315	
Basket, James	640	102	1	15 Dec 1779	33	281	69
Basket, James	68	24	26	20 Sep 1779	38	271	68
Bass, Jacob	640	39	41	20 Sep 1779	38	286	199
Bledso, Rush	640	54	56	12 Feb 1779	38	301	137
Brock, William	400	86	88	12 Feb 1779	38	333	98
Brogden, William	145	71	73	12 Feb 1779	38	318	143
Carr, Moses	23	16	18	20 Sep 1779	38	263	185
Collins, Michael	552	64	66	12 Feb 1779	38	311	16
Cook, Thomas	38	72	74	12 Feb 1779	38	319	104
Darnal, Charles	592	55	57	12 Feb 1779	38	302	188
Darnold, William	640	62	64	12 Feb 1779	38	309	80
Denson, William	300	79	81	12 Feb 1779	38	326	3
Denson, William	640	76	78	12 Feb 1779	38	323	1
Denson, William	260	42	44	12 Feb 1779	38	289	2
Denton, James	640	17	19	20 Sep 1779	38	264	177
Devaney, Jinkins	180	43	45	12 Feb 1779	38	290	117
Dinson, Edmund	640	78	80	12 Feb 1779	38	325	15
Dixon, Zachariah	640	66	68	12 Feb 1779	38	313	133
Dixon, Zachariah	200	53	55	12 Feb 1779	38	300	134
Dorsey, Calep	640	15	17	20 Sep 1779	38	262	108
Dorsey, Solomon	47	29	31	20 Sep 1779	38	276	67
Edwards, John	575		01				70
Ellington, John	611	26	28	20 Sep 1779	38	273	151
Ellis, Benjamin	450	101	103	12 Feb 1779	38	348	146
Elliss, William	320	49	51	12 Feb 1779	38	296	147
Ferrell, Bryon	300	94	96	12 Feb 1779	38	341	122
Fitts, Henry	164	63	65	12 Feb 1779	38	310	145
Fleming, Baley	546	90	92	12 Feb 1779	38	337	39
Freeman, Bridges	620	21	23	20 Sep 1779	38	268	222
Freeman, Edward	640	5	7	20 Sep 1779	38	252	125
Freeman, Edward	200	44	46	12 Feb 1779	38	291	126
Garriott, Matthew	343	50	52	12 Feb 1779	38	297	135
Goodloe, Robert	324	46	48	12 Feb 1779	38	293	140
Green, William	185	59	61	12 Feb 1779	38	306	17
Haggard, French	359	36	38	20 Sep 1779	38	283	208
Hawkins, John Jr	30	88	90	12 Feb 1779	38	335	57
Hawkins, Joseph	640	52	54	12 Feb 1779	38	299	50
Hawkins, Philemon, Junr	640	35	37	20 Sep 1779	38	282	61
Hawkins, Philemon, Junr	436	51	53	12 Feb 1779	38	298	62
Hensell, William	437	31	33	20 Sep 1779	38	278	192
Hill, Benjamin	600	2	4	20 Sep 1779	38	249	107
Hill, Henry, Jr.	293	57	59	12 Sep 1779	38	304	110
Hill, James	50	47	49	12 Feb 1779	38	294	190
Jeffreys, David	640	22	24	20 Sep 1779	38	269	142
Jeffreys, Osburn	140	7	9	20 Sep 1779	38	254	30
Jeffreys, Osburn	640	8	10	20 Sep 1779	38	255	28
Jeffreys, Osburn	500	3	5	20 Sep 1779	38	250	31
Jeffreys, Osburn	640	92	94	12 Feb 1779	38	339	26
Jeffreys, Osburn	80	10	12	20 Sep 1779	38	257	

Jeffreys, Simon	354	30	32	20 Sep 1779	38	277	19
Jeffreys, William	640	20	22	20 Sep 1779	38	267	95
Joiner, Moses	79	23	25	20 Sep 1779	38	270	263
Jones, James	112	18	20	20 Sep 1779	38	265	152
Jones, Roger	700	34	36	20 Sep 1779	38	281	240
Kimbell, Benjamin	600	65	67	12 Feb 1779	38	312	50
Lancaster, John	640	38	40	20 Sep 1779	38	285	200
Lewis, Nathaniel	62	14	16	20 Sep 1779	38	261	228
Lunceford, Limon	300	91	93	12 Feb 1779	38	338	107
Macon, John	194	96	98	12 Feb 1779	38	343	34
Mangum, Joseph	89	11	13	20 Sep 1779	38	258	206
Mathis, William	400	19	21	20 Sep 1779	38	266	207
May, John	300	70	72	12 Feb 1779	38	317	64
McGuffee, Lucy	129	93	95	12 Feb 1779	38	340	53
McLemore, Adkin	500	75	77	12 Feb 1779	38	322	40
McLemore, Adkin	247	25	27	20 Sep 1779	38	272	41
Mclemore, Young	202	41	43	12 Feb 1779	38	288	23
Mclemore, Young	640	27	29	20 Sep 1779	38	374	21
Merrett, Silvanus	263	4	6	20 Sep 1779	38	251	86
Merritt, James	413	103	2	15 Dec 1779	33	282	103
Merritt, Joseph	382	99	101	12 Feb 1779	38	346	102
Morris, James	417	81	83	12 Feb 1779	38	328	186
Murphrey, James	110	89	91	12 Feb 1779	38	336	148
Nickolson, James	419	12	14	20 Sep 1779	38	259	27
Pennell, John	60	98	100	12 Feb 1779	38	345	109
Perry, Ephraim	640	80	82	12 Feb 1779	38	327	82
Rachel, Ralph	640	60	62	12 Feb 1779	38	307	84
Raley, Andred	490	67	69	12 Feb 1779	38	314	97
Ransom, James	100	87	89	12 Feb 1779	38	334	193
Richards, John	361	48	50	12 Feb 1779	38	295	89
Richards, William	174	85	87	12 Feb 1779	38	332	88
Richardson, Edward	200	6	8	20 Sep 1779	38	253	73
Roland, Jesse Senr	78	95	97	12 Feb 1779	38	342	163
Rowland, Jesse	483	45	47	12 Feb 1779	38	292	83
Rowland, Jordan	416	9	11	20 Sep 1779	38	256	183
Salmon, Jonathan	155	1	3	20 Sep 1779	38	248	165
Self, Job	98	77	79	12 Feb 1779	38	324	198
Short, John	342	58	60	12 Feb 1779	38	305	56
Simmonds, John	300	56	58	12 Feb 1779	38	303	33
Smith, Abraham	200	37	39	20 Sep 1779	38	284	211
Smith, James	48	28	30	20 Sep 1779	38	275	124
Sorrell, George	640	97	99	12 Feb 1779	38	344	157
St. John, William	640	73	75	12 Feb 1779	38	320	129
Sumner, Jethro	670	32	34	20 Sep 1779	38	279	241
Thomas, John	334	82	84	12 Feb 1779	38	329	91
Thorn, Thomas	640	33	35	20 Sep 1779	38	280	131
Thornton, Roger	53	13	15	20 Sep 1779	38	260	212
Truelove, William	432	69	71	12 Feb 1779	38	316	81
Walker, Richard	21	84	86	12 Feb 1779	38	331	87
Ward, Benjamin	120	40	42	20 Sep 1779	38	287	38
Williams, Joseph	567	61	63	12 Feb 1779	38	308	158
Wright, Joseph	640	74	76	12 Feb 1779	38	321	128
Young, Thomas	640	100	102	12 Feb 1779	38	347	141

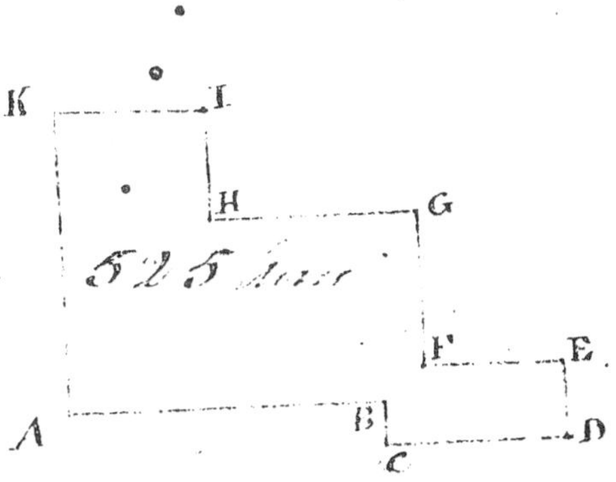

File #01

K I

H G

Scale 200 pole in an Inch 525 Acres

F E

A B D

C

Sept 19. 1778 Surveyed for John Edwards the following Tract of Land Lying in Bute County on Bear Swamp Begining at a Red Oak Seawels Corner Thence E° Along his line 202 p. to a W Oak Huckabys Cor Thence S° Along his line 38 p. to a Hick his Cor Thence E° Along his line 166 p. to a Pine Burres Cor Then N° along Burres line 66 Poles to a Hick on Seawels line Thence SW Along his line 126 p. to a post Oak his Cor Thence Along his line N° 140 p. to a post Oak Tats Cor Thence W along his line 190 pole to a pine his Cor Thence N° Along his line 100 pole to a post Oak Colliers Cor Thence W. Along his line 130 pole to a red Oak on his line Thence to the first Station Containing Five Hundred and Twenty Five Acres

Wm Solomon
Moses Gordon } CC
Cha Cass

Joseph Hawkins Sur.

Laid Down by a scale of two hundred pole [illegible] Creek

Surveyd August 24th 1778 for [illegible] 640 acres of land according to the above plan lying in Bute County on the waters of linches Creek & sandy Creek Beginning at a post oak In Hawkins line at the letter a thence E 132 poles to b to a hickrey at b thence N 115 poles to a [illegible] oak at c thence E 120 poles to a white oak d thence N 292 poles to a Black [illegible] at e thence West across two small Branches of sandy Creek & on of linches Creek 366 to a white oak at f thence S 134 poles to a stake In hawkins line at g thence E by his line 120 poles to a stake at h thence S to the Beginning

by [illegible] Hawkins

Charles [illegible]
Curtis Richards
Sw Ch. Car.

by

File #2

Laid Down by a scale
of two hundred poles to
an Inch

Surveyed August 25th 1778 for Jas Merritt
413 acres of land according to the above plan
lying in Bute County on Both sides Lynches
Creek Beginning on a Red Oak at letter A thence
So 324 crosses Lynches Creek to a hickory in Hawkins line at b thence
By his line S 80 Wt 125 to a hick. pine in ___ line at
C thence No 289 poles to a Black Jack at D thence
Wt 90 poles to a pine at E thence No ___
142 poles to a Black Jack at f thence E 215
poles to a Red Oak at G thence to the first
Station

Pines Weldon
&
Charles a Jew
Ch Carr

} by Joseph Hawkins C.S.

Page 5

File #3

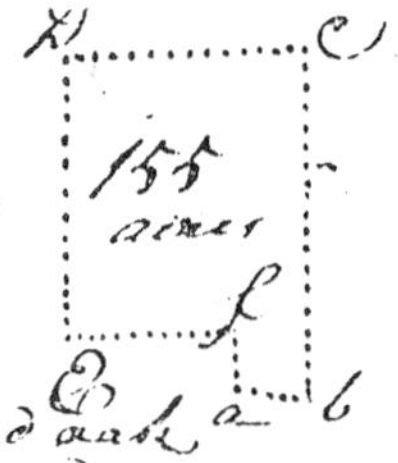

Plotted By a Scale of Two Hundred pole to an Inch

Decr 12th 1778 Surveyed for Jonathan Salmon 155 Acres of Land Agreeable to the annext plan Lying In Bute County on the Waters of hawtree Beginning at a Red oak at the Settle a thence by Sturdivants Line No 80 East 43 pole to a pine on Ballards line thence by sd line North 210 pole to a pine thence by Davis line West 142 pole to a hickory on the No side of Branch of hawtree thence By Jones line Along sd Branch So 164 pole to a hickory thence By Benjn Jones line East 96 pole to a white oak thence So 36 pole to the first Station

155 acres

Peter Jackson
Samuel Reel } Ch. Car.

Wm Christmas Surv

File #4

Plotted by a scale of Two hundred pole to an Inch

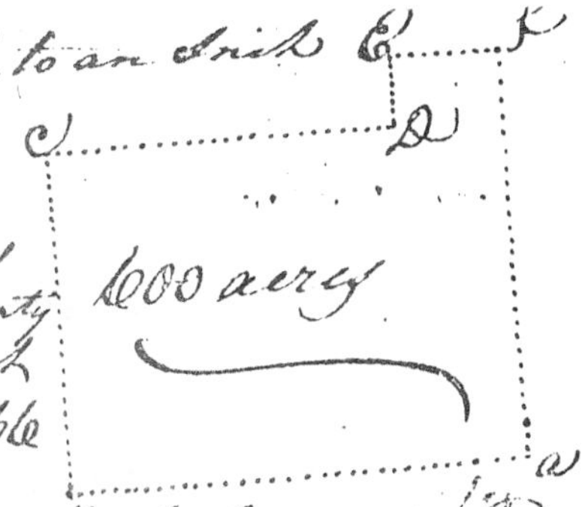

November 25th 1778 Surveyed for Benjn Hill 600 acres of Land of Land agreeable to the annexed plan Lying In Bute County on the No side Sandy Creek Beginning at a Black Oak at the Letter a thence East 366 pole to a white oak thence by murfreys line So 272 pole to murfreys Corner a pine thence by Parsons & fosters line West 282 pole to a pine thence So .. pole to a Red oak hills Corner thence by hills & Goodwins line West .. pole to a hickory thence by hills & Doziers line .. No to the first Station

Wm Christmas dsur

Thos Hogg & Jacob Waddel } Sw Ch Car

600 acres

File #5

Decemb 19th 1778 200 Do to an Inch

Then Surveyed for Osborn Jeffreys 500 Acres of Land lying in Bute County on ye South side of Cedar Creek Joing the lines of Osborn Jeffreys & David Jeffreyses lines Beginning at pine on the west side of the Road leading from the Mill to ye falls of Nuse thence N 160 poles to a pine thence E 48 poles to a pine thence N 40 poles to his Corner pine thence E 60 poles to a pine & Hickory thence N 90 poles to a White Oak thence E 144 poles to a White Oak thence S 230 poles to a Red Oak thence E 62 poles to a pine thence S 131 poles to a pine thence W 155 poles to a White Oak thence N 110 poles to White Oak thence W 160 poles to ye Beginning

Simon Jeffreys
Wm ...
} Chane Carriers

Pr me John Dent Dep Sur

File #7

August 27th 1778 } Plotted by the Scale of 200 Poles to an Inch

Then Surveyed for Edward Freem 640 Acres of Land Lying in the County of Bute on the Waters of Crooked Creek Begining at a Red Oak on A Tom bush branch Willis Perrys Corner thence E 25 Poles to a Spanish Oak thence S 324 Poles to a pine thence W 220 Poles to Hickory thence N 123 Poles to a White Oak thence W 112 Poles to a Stone thence N 228 Poles to a Red Oak thence E 310 Poles to a Red Oak in Perrys line thence S 40 Poles to ye first Station

Pr. me John Dent Dep: Surv. for Joseph Hawkins Sur.

Bryon Fried } Chain Carriers
Wm Freeman }

E 310 Poles; N 228 Poles; S 324 P; W 112 P; N 123; W 220 P; A 640

File #6

Plotted by a scale of Two Hundred pole to Inch

Decr. 5th 1778 Surveyed for Silvanus Merrett 263 acres of Land agreeable to the above plan Lying in Bute County on Stonehouse Creek Beginning at Holomons Corner a Black Oak at the Letter A thence By his line East 156 pole to Walkers Corner a hickory on the West side Stonehouse thence by Walkers line across Stonehouse Sth 270 pole to a Stake thence by Pettersons line Wt. 156 pole to a Red oak thence by Holomans line No. 270 pole to the first station

Newit Harris & Wm Williams } Sw. Ch. Carrs.

by Wm Chrismas Survr.

a B; 263 acres; D C

File #9

Jan[?] 12 1779 Then Surveyed for Osborn Jeffreys 140 Acres of Land lying in Bute County on [illegible] of Davises Creek [illegible] own lines Beginning [illegible] thence [illegible] poles to a pine thence W 66 poles to a pine [illegible] thence S 280 poles to a pine thence W 62 poles to a thence N 320 poles to a thence E 130 poles to y Beginning

Simon Jeffreys } Chane
Wm May } Carriers

[illegible] me John Dent
Dept Surv

for [illegible]

File #8

November y 13th 1778 Then Surveyed for Edward [illegible] 200 Acres of Land lying in Bute County on y waters of Red Bud Creek Beginning at a White Oak & two Red Oaks thence N 238 poles to gum on Red bud Creek thence E 120 po to a [illegible] in Collins line thence N 24 po to a Red Oak thence E 20 po to Hickory in Collins line thence N 214 po to a black Jack thence W 130 poles to y Beginning

Wm [illegible] } Chane Carriers
Marcus Gilham }

Pr me John Dent Dept
for [illegible]

December 18 1778
200 poles to an Inch
Then Surveyed for Osborn
Jeffrey 640 Acres of Land
lying in Bute County on ye
Watters of Rays Creek & Davises
Creek Joining his own lines
& David Jeffreys lines Beg
inning in David Jeffreys line
at a Red Oak on the south side of
the said Creek thence N 121 pole to a Red & White Oak
thence W 100 po to a White Oak thence N 212 po to three
White Oaks thence E 180 po to a pine thence N 160 po ..
a pine thence W 52 poles to his Corner Red Oak in Ba
sses line thence S 62 poles with the sd Basses line
to Basses Corner White Oak thence W 340 po to Rays
Creek to a Red Oak & ash thence up ye sd Creek S 95
poles to a Hickory Maple & ash in sd Jeffreys line
thence by his line S 62 po to a pine thence S 341 po
to a White Oak thence to ye Beginning ——

Benjamin May } Chane
Wm Roberts } Carriers

pr me John Dew
Depl Sur
for Wm Christmas

Laid Down by a scale of two hundred pole to an Inch

Dec 1st 1779 surveyd for Cordan Roland 416 acres of Land agreeable to the above plan Lying In bute County on the waters of falling Creek Beginning at a stake In purcons line at the lettr a thence by Weldons line East 123 pole to a Sassifras In Isaac Rawlands line thence by sd line So East 277 pole to a stake In Doolings line thence by sd line West 60 pole to three white oaks thence by his other line 132 pole across falling Creek to a white oak thence West 130 pole to a pine thence N 130 pole to a white thence East 100 pole to a Red oak purcons Corner thence by his Line No 327 pole to the first Station

Richard acock
Wm Mathis { Sw Ch Car. Wm Christmas S

File #11

File #12

Jan 12 1779 by 100 poles to an Inch
Then Surveyed for Simon Jeffreys 80 Acres of Land Lying Between Parsons Creek & Sedar Creek Bounded all Round by his own lines Beginning at a pine thence N 132 poles to a pine thence E 100 poles to a pine thence S 90 poles to a pine & Hickory thence W 5 po to a thence S 40 poles to a pine & Hickory thence W 95 poles to ye first station

Simon Jeffreys
Wm May { Chane Carriers } Vme John Dent Dep Surr for Wm Christmas S

File #13

Plotted by a scale of Two Hundred pole to An Inch

November 23rd 1778 Surveyd for Joseph Mangum 189 acres of Land agreeable to the anneat plan Lying In Bute County on the waters of Martins Creek Beginning at Christmass Corner a white oak at the Lett. a thence by Balls line No. 75 pole to a Black Oack thence by Line W. 378 pole to a Red oak In the Cott line thence by Falkners line S. 20 W. 78 pole to a stake On D. Christmass line thence East By D. line ~~line~~ to the first Station

189 acres

Sa. Cooper
&
Martin Dickerson } Sw Ch Car. by Wm. Christmas S.

File #15

Plotted by a scale of Two Hundred pole to an Inch

53 acres

Dec. 23rd 1778 Surveyd for Roger Thornton 53 acres of Land agreeable to the anneat plan Lying In Bute County on the waters of Weavers Creek Beginning at a Red oak In houses Line at the Lett. a thence by ward's line No. 42 pole to his Corner a post oak thence by his other Line Creek 202 pole to a Red oak thence S. 42 pole to a stake In houses line thence by his Line W. to the first Station

Wm. Thornton
&
Henry Thornton } Sw Ch Car. by Wm. Christmas Survr.

Plotted by a scale of two hundred pole to an Inch

December 4th 1779 Surveyed for Samuel Nicholson 419 acres of Land agreeable to the Act(?) Warrant lying in the County of [illegible] on the Waters of Stonehouse & Rub Quarter Creeks on both sides Eatons Road & Halifax Road Beginning at a White oak Solomons Corner at the [illegible] thence by his line [illegible] 306 pole to a black Jack thence by his other line S° 20 pole to a Black oak on the N° side Eatons Road thence [illegible] 14 pole to a Black oak thence N° 125 pole to an [illegible] in Kelleys line thence his line [illegible] 273 pole to a Red oak thence his other line N° 320 pole to a white oak thence by Durhams line East 20 pole to a Red oak thence by Riggans line [illegible] pole to a white oak thence his other line [illegible] 166 pole to a Red oak thence by Hedges line [illegible] 79 pole to a Gum on a branch of Stonehouse thence his other line [illegible] Creek 22 pole to a white oak thence by Nicholsons line [illegible] pole to a Red oak thence by Harris line [illegible] 168 pole to a hickory thence his other line [illegible] to the first Station

Archey Nicholson
Davis Nicholson

Sw. C. C. by Wm Christmas

File #16

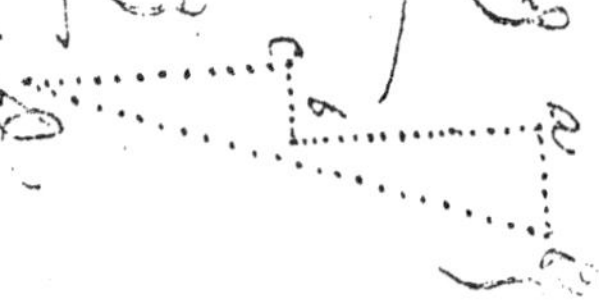

Plotted by a scale of Two Hundred pole to y^e Inch

February 2^d 1775 Surveyed for Nathaniel Lewis 6 acres of Land agreeable to the annexed Plan lying in Burke County on the Waters of Sinchers Creek Beginning at [illegible] a white oak at the Letter a thence by Crabs Yates line N^o [illegible] 14 pole to a pine thence by his Line East 45 pole to a Red oak thence by Haggards line N 24 E 60 pole across a Branch of Sinchers Creek to a pine In the County line thence by sd. Line S 80 W 79 pole to a Stake On the [illegible] Huckabys line thence by sd line East to the first Station

Hezekiah Wright
Richard Wright } S C C [illegible] Wm Christmas

a b c D

File #18

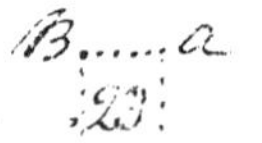

Plotted by a scale of two hundred pole to an Inch

February 1st 1775 Surveyed for Moses Carr 23 acres of Land agreeable to the annexed plan lying In Burke County on the waters of Kings Creek Beginning at Woolleys Corner a Red oak at the letter a thence East 45 pole to Smiths Corner a Red oak thence N^o by his line 81 pole to a hickory In Morris line thence by his line W 45 pole to a Red oak thence by his other line N 81 pole to the first Station

Thos. Woolley
Jno. Powell } Sw^n C. Carr.

by Wm Christmas D.S.

B a 23 D

Platted by a scale of two hundred
Pole to an Inch

Q · · · P · R · · M · B · a · C · D

640 acres L

November 26th 1773 Surveyed for
Caleb Dorsey 640 acres of Land
Agreeable to the annexed plan Lying In Bute County
on the waters of Sandy Creek Beginning at Watleys
Corner In Surveys line a pine at the S. W. (a) thence By
Watleys line East 248 pole to a white oak thence by
his other line No. 12 pole to a Red oak thence by
Myricks line East 138 pole to a white oak On
Williamsons line thence by his line S. 20. East
30 pole to a Black Jack thence by his other line East
72 pole to a stake thence S. 173 pole to a stake On
Benja. Hills line thence by his line W. 354 pole to
a Black Jack thence by his other line S. 59 pole to
a Black Jack Thos. Hills Corner thence by his line W.
116 pole to a Red oak On Howells line thence by his
line No. 132 to a Red oak thence by his other line
W. 12 pole to a Red oak thence by Powers line No. 118
pole to the first Station

Solomon Dorsey
Jno. Myrick } Sco. Ch. Car. by Wm. Christmas Surv.

Plotted by a scale of two hundred pole to an Inch

January 29th 1779 Surveyed for James Denton,
640 acres of Land agreeable to the annexed
Plan Lying In Bute County on Both
Sides Little Creek Beginning at
a Rock oak In Dentons line at the
Little Cr thence by his & Hackneys line
East 302 to a white on the No. side Weavers Creek
Coining house S° 5° East 135 pole to wards Corner a
White oak on the Wt. Side said Creek thence by his line
W. 155 pole to a pine thence his other line S°. 300 along
Little [illegible] Creek to a Red oak thence by Millers line W,
72 pole to a pine thence N°. 155 pole to a pine thence
W. 205 pole to a Red oak thence N°. 203 pole to a Black
Oack thence East 115 pole to a white oak thence N°.
across Little Creek to the first Station

James House } Sw Ch Ckr by Wm Christmas Surv
& Simon Beckham }

Plotted by a scale of two hundred pole to An Inch

Dec. 10th 1778 Surveyed for James Jones 112 acres of Land a Greeable to the above plan Lying in Bute County on the waters of hawtree Beginning at a hickory Dickins Corner at the letter a thence N°. 36 pole to a white oak thence East 58 pole to a white oak thence By Long line N° 88 pole to a Black Jack thence East 142 pole to a Hickory thence S° 168 pole across a Branch of hawtree to a hickory thence N° 45d W° across Sd Branch to the first Station

David King
Jn. Clinton } Ch Carr. — by Wm Christmas Surv.

File # 20

File #21

Plotted by a scale of 200 pole to an Inch

Dec. 1st 1779 Surveyed for Wm Halifax 400 acres of land a Greeable to the annexed plan Lying In Bute County on the waters of hawtree & falling Creek Beginning ~~[illegible]~~ at a Black Jack In Davis line at the letter a thence by Halifax line N° 25d East 246 pole to a poplar on the Sd side falling Creek thence up the Creek S° 70d W° 70 pole to a poplar In Dowling line thence his line S° 48d W. 158 pole to a white oak thence his other line N° 160 pole to a white oak thence West 183 pole to a pine thence S° 270 pole across Hawtree to a pine In Davis line thence his line East ~~[illegible]~~ 225 pole across Sd Creek to the first Station

Emma Mathis
Thos. Blanchet } Ch C by Wm Christmas Surv.

File #23

Novemb^r^ 12 1778 Then Surveyed for Bridges Freeman 620 Acres of Land lying in Bute County on Andrews Creek Beginning at a Red Oak Hartsfields Corner thence E 52 poles to a pine in Mannocks line thence N 384 P^o^ to a Red Oak his Corner thence W 250 P^o^ to a pine thence N 150 P^o^ to a pine thence W 350 P^o^ by his line to a Spanish Oak Jones Corner thence S 194 P^o^ with his line to a Red Oak thence E 210 P^o^ to a White Oak thence S 20 P^o^ to a White Oak thence E 320 P^o^ to a Hickory then S 320 P^o^ to y^e^ Beginning

Henry Freeman } Chain Carriers
John Freeman }

200 poles to an Inch

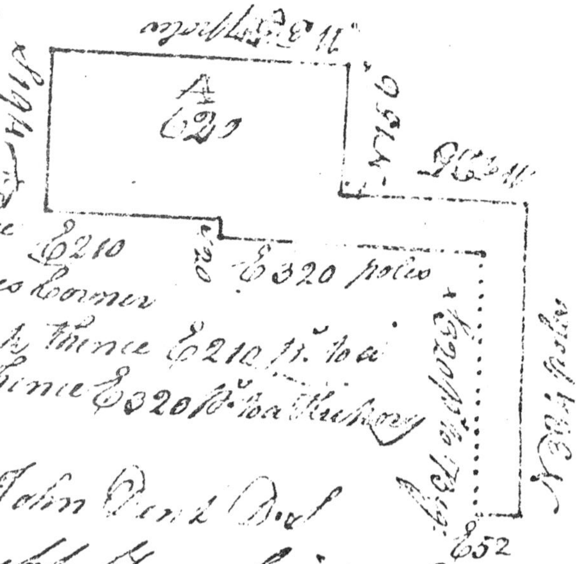

W 350 poles — N 150 — W 250 — N 384 poles — E 52 — E 320 poles — S 320 poles — 20 — E 210 — S 194

A 620

Pr. John Dent D.S. for Joseph Hawkins Sur

File #22

Sep^t^ 29th 1778 } Surveyed for William Jeffreys 640 Acres of Land Lying in Bute County on ye N Side of Little River Beginning at a white Oak on the S Side of Buck Branch Running thence W 260 Poles to a post oak thence N 40 Poles to a Black Jack thence W 74 Poles to a Jack oak thence N 345 Poles to a pine thence E 334 Poles to a black Jack thence S 385 to the first Station

John Richards & William Moody } Chain Carriers

P^r^ Me John Dent DS for Joseph Hawkins Sur

P^r^ 200 poles to an Inch

E 334 P^o^ — S 385 poles — W 260 — N 345 P^o^ — 40 — 74

A 640

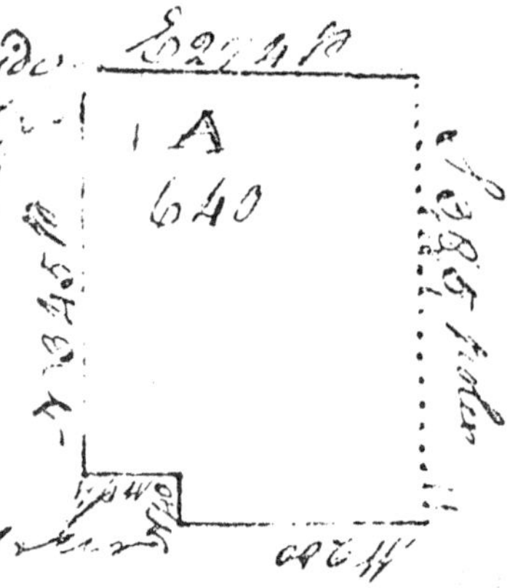

File #24

Decem. 18. 1778

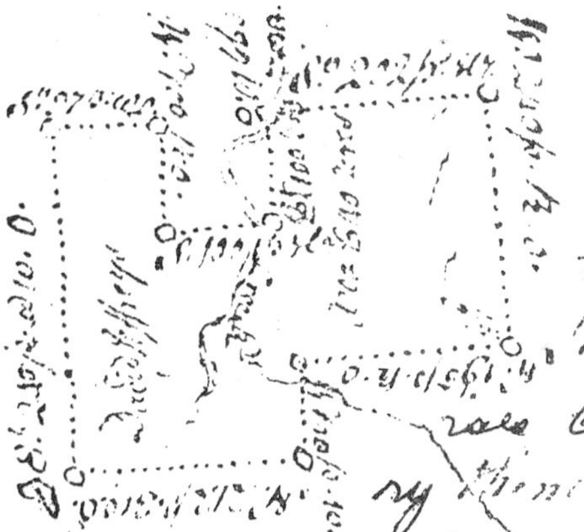

Then Surveyed for David Jeffreys 640 Acres of Land lying in Bute County on both sides of Dawses Creek Beginning at a White Oak on Dawses Creek thence S202 poles to a Hickory thence W340 poles to a Red Oak thence N195 poles to a Red Oak thence W100 poles to a White Oak thence N212 poles to 3 Oaks thence E340 poles to a White Oak thence S97 poles to a White Oak thence W100 poles to a Red Oak thence S100 poles to a Hickory thence E100 poles to ye Beginning —— P. me John Dent Dept Survr

Benjamin May } Chain
Wm Roberts } Carriers

for Wm Christmas C.S.

File #25

Jany 24 1779

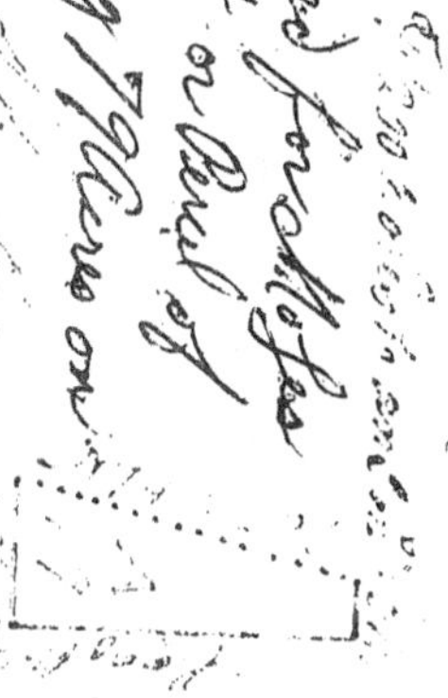

Then Surveyed for Moses Joiner a tract or Parcel of Land Containg 79 Acres on the [illegible] Brookes [illegible] Creek Beginning at a Maple on said Creek thence N34 Poles to a pine Wm Perrys Corner thence E220 poles to a pine at Ferrils Corner thence S90 poles to a Maple on the Run of the sd Creek thence up the Various Courses of the Creek to ye first Station N74 W236 poles ——

Henry Freeman
Wm Joiner
Chain Carriers

P. me John Dent D.S.

for [illegible] C.S.

Plotted by a Scale of Two Hundred pole to an Inch

January 25th 1779 Surveyed for James Barkett 68 acres of Land agreeable to the Annexed plan lying in Bute County Beginning at a Black Jack In Barketts line at the letter a thence by s^d line N° 38 pole to a post oak thence N° 85^d W^t 69 pole to a Black Jack on the S^o side Called Road thence up the Road S^o 68^d W^t 172 pole thence S^o 52^d W^t 10 pole thence East to the first Station

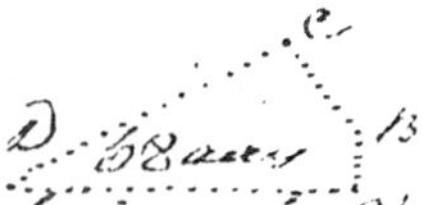

68 acres

Howel Cooper
&
Wm Duty

Sw Ch. Carr. by Wm Christmas

File #26

File #27

Plotted by a Scale of Two Hundred pole to an Inch

November 21st 1778 Surv^d for Atkins McLemore 247 acres of land agreeable to the Annexed plan lying In bute County on Lees branch Beginning at his own Corner a white on Lees branch at the letter a thence up the said branch N. 30^d W^t 100 pole thence N° 130 pole to hendersons Corner a pine Course Continued by his line 68 pole to a Red oak On hawkins, line thence By s^d line E^t 100 pole to a hickory thence S^o 168 pole to a white oak McLemores Corner thence by his line S^o 30 W^t to the first Station

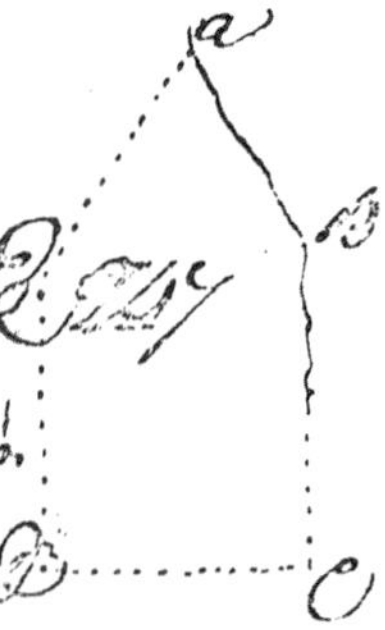

247

Sugar McLemore
&
Little Bury White

Sw Ch. Car^a by Wm Christmas Sur

platted by a scale of Two Hundred pole to the inch

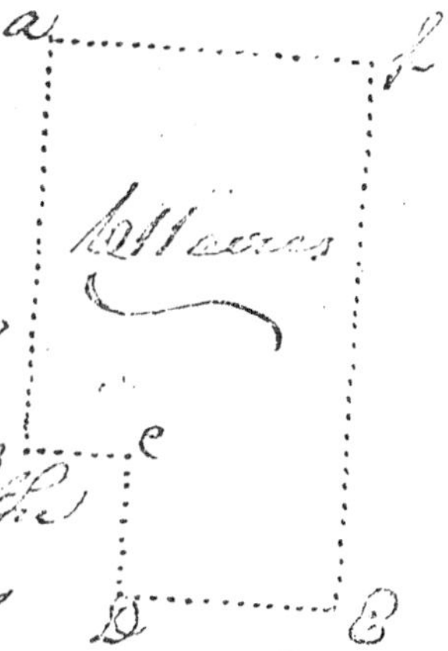

March 10th 1778 Surveyed for John Clenton 640 acres of land agreeable to the annexed plan lying in Wilkes County Between Mulberry & Smiths Creek Beginning at a Red oak in the Virginia Line at the letter A thence by Davis Gunnells line South 320 pole to a Red oak thence by Kings line East 180 pole to a white oak thence by his other line South 103 to a Black Jack thence by Conner line East 170 pole to a white oak thence by Dickins & Daves North 428 pole to a stake in the County line thence by sd line West to the first Station

Henry Tucker
William Roberson } S.C.C. & by Wm Christmas Survr

File #28

platted by a scale of Two hundred pole to an inch

November 21st 1778 Survd for Atkin McLemore 247 acres of land agreeable to the annexed plan lying in Wilkes County on Deer branch Beginning at his own Corner a white on Deer branch at the letter A thence up the said branch N 30 West 140 pole thence N 130 pole to Hendersons Corner a pine Course Continued by his line 108 pole to a Red oak on Hawkins's line thence by sd line S 160 pole to a hickory thence S 103 pole to a white oak McLemores Corner thence by his line S 80 West to the first Station

Sugar McLemore
&
Little Berry Mills } S.Ch. Carr by Wm Christmas Sur

File #27

File #29

Plotted by a scale of 200 pole to an inch

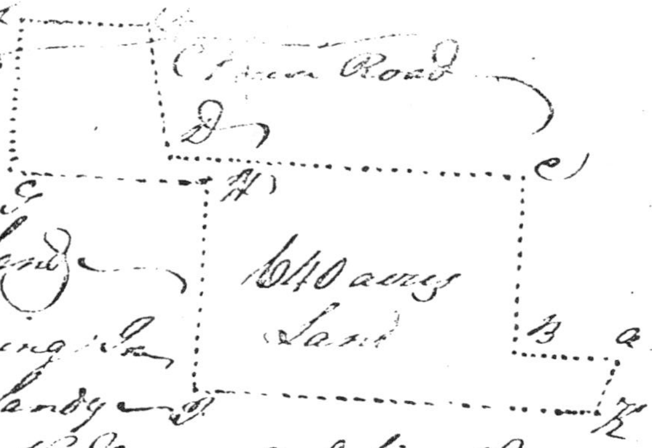

640 acres Land

Road

January 27th 1779 Surveyed for Young McLemore 640 acres of Land Agreeable to the annexed plan lying in Bute County on the waters of Sandy Creek Beginning at a Red oak in the Granville Line thence by Brooks line East 107 pole to a pine thence by his other line No. 150 pole to a post oak on Christmas line thence his line East 243 pole to his corner [illegible] Continued 129 pole to a Black Jack thence So. 13 East 136 pole to a Red oak in Nichols line thence his ~~line~~ by Millers line East 30 pole to a pine thence No. across the old Courthouse Road 155 pole to a pine thence Wt. 205 pole to a Red oak thence No. 208 pole to a Black Jack thence Wt. 412 pole to a white oak in the Granville line thence by sd. line So. 20 Wt. 100 pole to the first Station

Thomas Christmas & Moses Fortner } SCC. by Wm Christmas Survr.

File #31

Plotted by a Scale of Two Hundred pole In an Inch

Decr 22nd 1779 Surveyed for Solomon Dowey 47 acres of Land a Greeable to the annext plan Lying In Bute County on the No Side Sandy Creek Beginning at Vatoms Corner a Redoak at the Settl a thence by his Line No 104 pole to a Stake In Seay Doweys line thence by his S Gibbs lines West 90 pole to a Dead white oake on the No Bank of Sandy Creek thence Down the Various Courses thereof to the first Station

Eleay Dowey

Adel Mosley { Sur, C. Cont. by Wm. Christmas

A 47 C B

File #30

Plotted by a Scale of Two Hundred pole to an Inch

february 2nd 1779 Surveyed for James Smith 48 acres of Land a Greeable to the annext plan Lying In Bute County Beginning at Wm Smiths Corner a Redoak at the Settl a thence West 32 pole to a popular In Stones line thence by S line No 244 pole to a white oak thence East thence by his line No 244 pole to a white oak In Smiths Line thence by his Each 38 pole to a white oak In Smiths Line thence by his Line Sou to the first Station

Thos Hellier & Jno Rackly { Sur, C. Carn by Wm Christmas Sworn

C D 48 acres B A

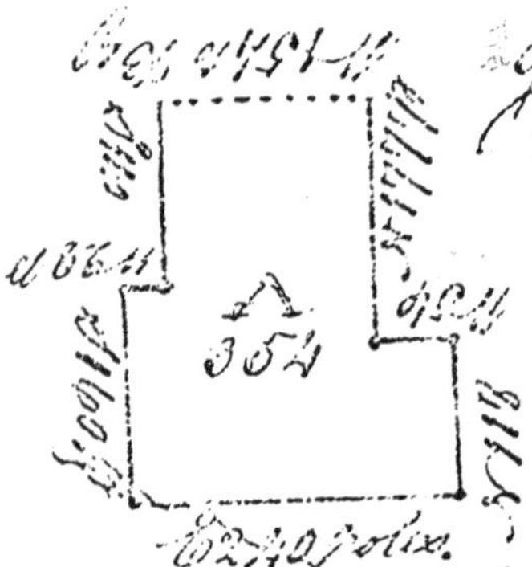

Jan.^ry 13 - 1779 — ℔ 200 poles to an Inch

Then Surveyed for Simon Jeffreys 354 acres of Land lying in Bute County on the North Side of Buffaloe Beginning at Davis his Corner pine thence E 140 po. to his own Corner pine thence N 28 po. to his own Corner pine thence S 100 poles to Mays line [illegible] Jeffreys to a Bay Bush thence E 240 poles with Mays line to a Red Oak thence thence N 113 po. to sd Jeffreys line & Coopers Corner pine thence by Coopers line W 56 po. to a pine thence N 177 po. to Wests line Now [illegible] thence W 157 poles to the Beginning —

Wm May } Chain
Tho. May } Carriers

Pr me John Dent D.S.
for Wm Christmas S—

File #32

Platted by a scale of Two Hundred pole to an Inch Decr 11th 1778 Surveyd for Wm Dennele 437 acres of Land Agreeable to the Annext plan Lying In Bute County on the Waters of Smiths Creek & Tomlones Mill Creek Beginning at a white oak at the Lett. A thence by Balia's line South 213 pole to a willow oak thence by nicholson's line West 232 pole to a hickory thence by Robertsons line North 316 pole to a white oak thence by Davis line East 133 pole to a white oak thence North 40 pole to a white oak thence East 102 pole to the first Station

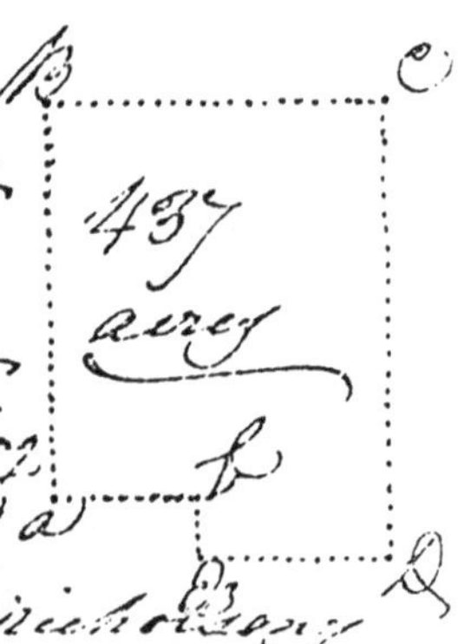

Wm Elenton
Jno King Robert } Chain Carrs

by Wm Christmas Survr

File #33

437 acres

Nicholsons & Clemons line

File #35

Plotted by a scale of two hundred pole to an Inch

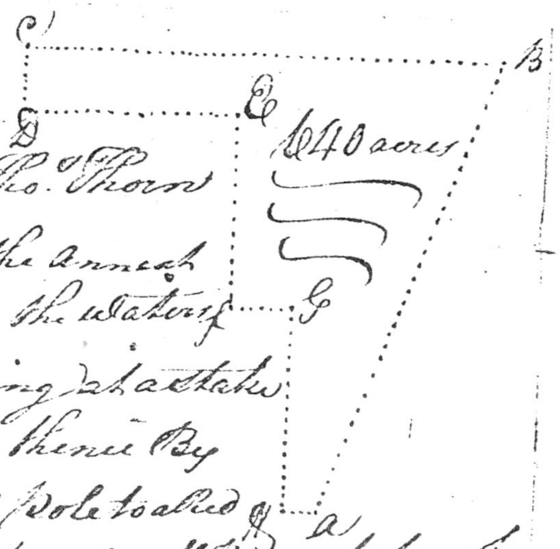

September 21st 1778 Surveyed for Thos. Thorn 640 acres of Land agreeable to the annexed plan Lying In Bute County on the waters of Weavers & Sandy Creeks Beginning at a stake In Cordons line at the lett. a thence By the Granville line So. 20d Wt. 540 pole to a Red oak thence East 540 pole across two Small Branches of Sandy Creek to a post oak on the S. side little Creek thence No. across Sd. Creek 70 pole to a post oak In Dentons line thence Wt. 242 pole to a post [illegible] thence by Williams's line No. 212 pole to Eatons Corner thence by his line Wt. 69 pole to a white oak thence No. 228 pole to a post [illegible] Cordons Corner thence by his line Wt. 38 pole to the first Station

Carrier William & Presly Thorn } Sw Ch Car. by Wm. Christmas D Survr. for Jos. Hawkins Survr.

A, B, C, D, E, G

640 acres

File #36

[illegible] by [illegible] of two hundred pole to a stake

February 3 1779 Surveyed for Roger Terry
700 acres of Land according to the annext
plan Lying in Burke County on the waters
of Brushy Creek Beginning at a White oak [illegible]
[illegible] line [illegible] thence East 170 pole
to a stake thence N° 119 pole to a [illegible] oak thence
East 100 pole to a pine on [illegible] line [illegible]
on a branch of Brushy Creek thence by [illegible] line
[illegible] line N° 467 pole along [illegible] branch of Brushy Creek
to a white oak thence by [illegible] line [illegible] 207 pole to a
White Oak thence N° 202 pole to a white oak thence
[illegible] 169 pole to a pine thence N° 227 pole to the first
Station

700 Acres

Jn° Hight } [illegible] Ch Carr. [illegible] Wm Christmas Surv.
Herbert Hight }

File #37

Plotted by a Scale of Two Hundred pole to an Inch
January 25th 1779 Surveyed for Philimon Hawkins Jr
640 acres of Land agreeable to the annexed
plan Lying In Bute County on the
Waters of fishing Creek Beginning
at a pine On the County Line at the
Sixth a thence East 143 pole to a pine
in Widow Bartlets line thence No by
sd line 231 pole along fishing Creek to a pine thence East
230 pole along sd Creek to a Stake thence by Dukes line
along sd Creek No 98 pole to a Red oak thence by his
other Line East 108 pole to a pine thence by James Bartlets
Line No 206 pole to a Black Oak thence Wt 200 pole to
Collins Road thence up the Road S 42 Wt 72 pole to the Cty
Line thence By sd line to the first Station

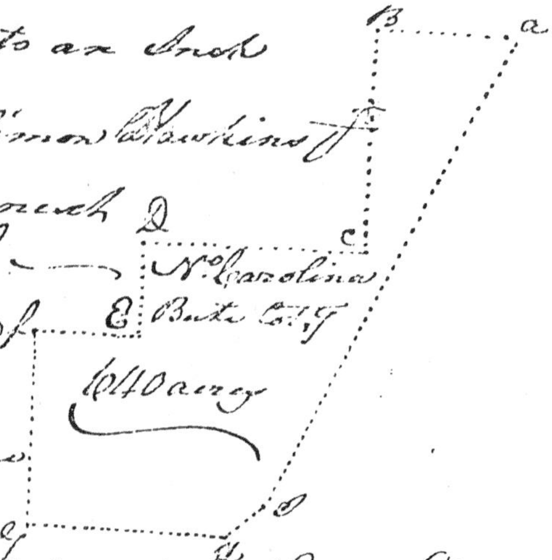

B a F D C
No Carolina
E Bute Cty
640 acres
G H

Howel Cooper
Wm Duke } Sw Ch Carr. by Wm Christmas Survr

Plotted by a Scale of Two Hundred — pole to an Inch —

February 8th 1779 Survey^d for French Haggard 359 acres of Land agreeable to the annexed plan lying in Butte County on the waters of Linches Creek Beginning at a Hickory on the County Line at the letter a thence by Smith's Line East 125 pole to pine thence by his other line No 182 pole to a pine thence by Finches Line East 198 pole along a Branch of Linches Creek to a maple thence by Jones Line S 175 pole to a white oak thence W 45 pole to a hickory on fullers line thence by his line No [illegible] pole to a Red oak thence W 183 pole to a pine thence S 180 pole to a hickory thence by merritts & Simons line W along a Branch of Buffaloe 240 pole to a stake on the County Line thence by s^d line to the first station

Thomas Hecum
Robert Lewis } Sw Ch Carr   by Wm Christmas Surv^r

File #39

Plotted by a scale of Two hundred po: to an Inch

November 27th 1778 Survey'd for Abraham Smith 200 acres of Land agreeable to the annexed plan Lying In Bute County Beginning at Merritts Corner a hickory at the letter a thence No 117 poles to a pine in [illegible] Rogers line thence by his line W 107 pole to a Red oak In the County line thence by sd line [illegible] pole to a post oak In Edwards line thence by his line [illegible] 112 pole to a post oak thence by his other line [illegible] 84 pole to a Hickory thence East 72 pole to a Corner of two lines thence S[illegible] 183 pole to a black Jack In Merretts ~~line thence~~ New line thence By sd line to the first Station

James Merritt }
Danl Edwards } Sw Ch Carr

Ays Wm Christmas S

g f e b 200 acres a c d

File #40

Plotted by a scale of two hundred pole to an Inch

Decr 5th 1779 Surveyd for John Lancaster 640 acres of Land Agreeable to the Annexed plan Lying In Bute County on Both sides Deep Creek Beginning at a pine In Capps line at the letter a thence by his line East 140 pole to a Red oak thence by Harris line No 243 pole to a white oak thence by his line East 90 poles to a Black Jack thence by Williams line No 340 pole to a Red oak on the aforementioned Creek thence up the meanders thereof S 60 W 100 po to a [illegible] Corner thence by his line W 130 pole to a white oak thence by Harris line S 243 poles to a Red oak thence his other line W 10 poles to a Red oak thence So to the first Station

Sterling Harris }
Jno Lancaster } Sw Ch Carr

Ays Wm Christmas Sur

g f 640 acres h b c d e

File #42

Plotted by a scale of two Hundred pole to an Inch

January 1st 1779 Surveyd for Benja. Ward 120 acres of Land Agreeable to the Annexed Plan lying In Bute County Beginning at a black Jack at the letter A thence by Perrys line S. 20 Wt. 24 pole to a Red oak thence S. 33 East 125 pole to a white oak thence S. 63 Wt. [illegible] pole to a White oak thence by Jarvis line N 28 Wt. 35 pole to a white oak thence by his other line S 65 Wt. 164 pole to a white oak thence N. 32 East 102 pole to a white oak thence N 36 Wt. 73 pole to a Red oak In Perrys line thence by his line East to the first Station

Thomas Cooper
Lewis Jank } Sw. Ch. Carrs. by Wm. Christmas S

File #41

Plotted by a scale of Two Hundred pole in an Inch

January 10th 1779 Surveyd for Jacob Day 640 acres of Land Agreeable to the above Plan lying In Bute County on the Waters of Sandy Creek Beginning at Gatlins Corner at the letter A thence By Tommy's line East 293 pole a long ye two Branches of Sandy Creek to a post oak thence By Davis line No. 350 pole to a post oak on the No. side Halifax Road thence Wt. 293 pole to a stake In Gatlins line thence By Sd. line S. to the first Station.

Benja. [illegible]
Daniel Duke } Sw. Ch. Carriers by Wm. Christmas Survr.

File #44

[illegible] Scale 200 p to an Inch –

200 Acres

July 11th 1778 Surveyed for Wm Denson the following tract of land lying in Burke County Cont. 200 Acres [illegible] [illegible] [illegible] [illegible] [illegible] thence [illegible] to a pine thence [illegible] [illegible] [illegible] thence [illegible] [illegible] Oak thence [illegible] Red Oak in his [illegible] [illegible] thence [illegible] along his line to a [illegible] Oak on [illegible] line thence to the first Station

[illegible] } Ch Car.
John [illegible] }

Joseph Hawkins

File #43

Said Draft By Scale of two Hundred pole to an Inch –

Surveyed July 30th 1778 for Young McLemore 200 acres of Land according to the Above plan lying In Burke County on the waters of Shoco Begt at Seth Williams's Corner a Black Oak at the Letter a thence by his line N 3° E 271 po to a pine at B thence N 87 E 142 pole to a post oak at C thence S 3° E 122 Pole to a pine at D E 100 pole to a Stake at E thence N 3° E 134 to a Red oak at F thence E 142 pole to a hickory bush on the N Side Shoco in McLemores line at G thence up the Various Courses of Shoco to the head at A thence W to the first Station

Elias Dorsey }
R Beckham } Sw Ch Car.

by Jos Hawkins

File #45

Laid down By ... of two hundred Pole to an Orch

Surveyed Sept 15th 1778 for ... Devaney 180 Acres of Land according to the above Plan Lying in Burke County on the waters of Buffaloe Beginning at Devaneys Corner on ... line a ... at the letter A thence By ... line ... 180 to Hawkins Corner a Red oak at B thence By Huckabays line ... pole to his Corner ... at C thence By ... line ... to Devaneys Corner a Black Oak at D thence By Devaneys line ... a Road by a Branch of Buffaloe to the first station

... Bragdon } Chain Carriers
Robert Galen }

J. Hawkins ...

File #46

Aug. the 27 1778

Then Surveyed for Edward Freeman 200 Acres of Land Lying in the County of Burke on the North side of the ... of Cedar Creek Beginning at a Red Oak in ... line thence ... poles to a White Oak thence ... to a Spanish Oak in ... line thence South 120 Poles to the Beginning

... 260 poles ...

... } Chain
Wm Freeman } Carriers

... me John ... Dep. Surv.
for Joseph Hawkins Surv.

File #47

[illegible] 1778 Then Surveyed for [illegible] 403 Acres of Land in the County of Kent in the [illegible] Creek Beginning at a [illegible] in [illegible] line thence [illegible] 100 p[o] to a pine thence [illegible] 100 p[o] to a Red Oak thence [illegible] 100 p[o] to a [illegible] in [illegible] line thence [illegible] p[o] to a pine thence [illegible] p[o] to a pine [illegible] thence [illegible] 140 p[o] to a post Oak thence [illegible] p[o] to a [illegible] Oak thence [illegible] p[o] to a [illegible] thence [illegible] p[o] to a White [illegible] Thence to first station

[illegible] Chain Carriers } [illegible] for Joseph Hawkins [illegible]

File #48

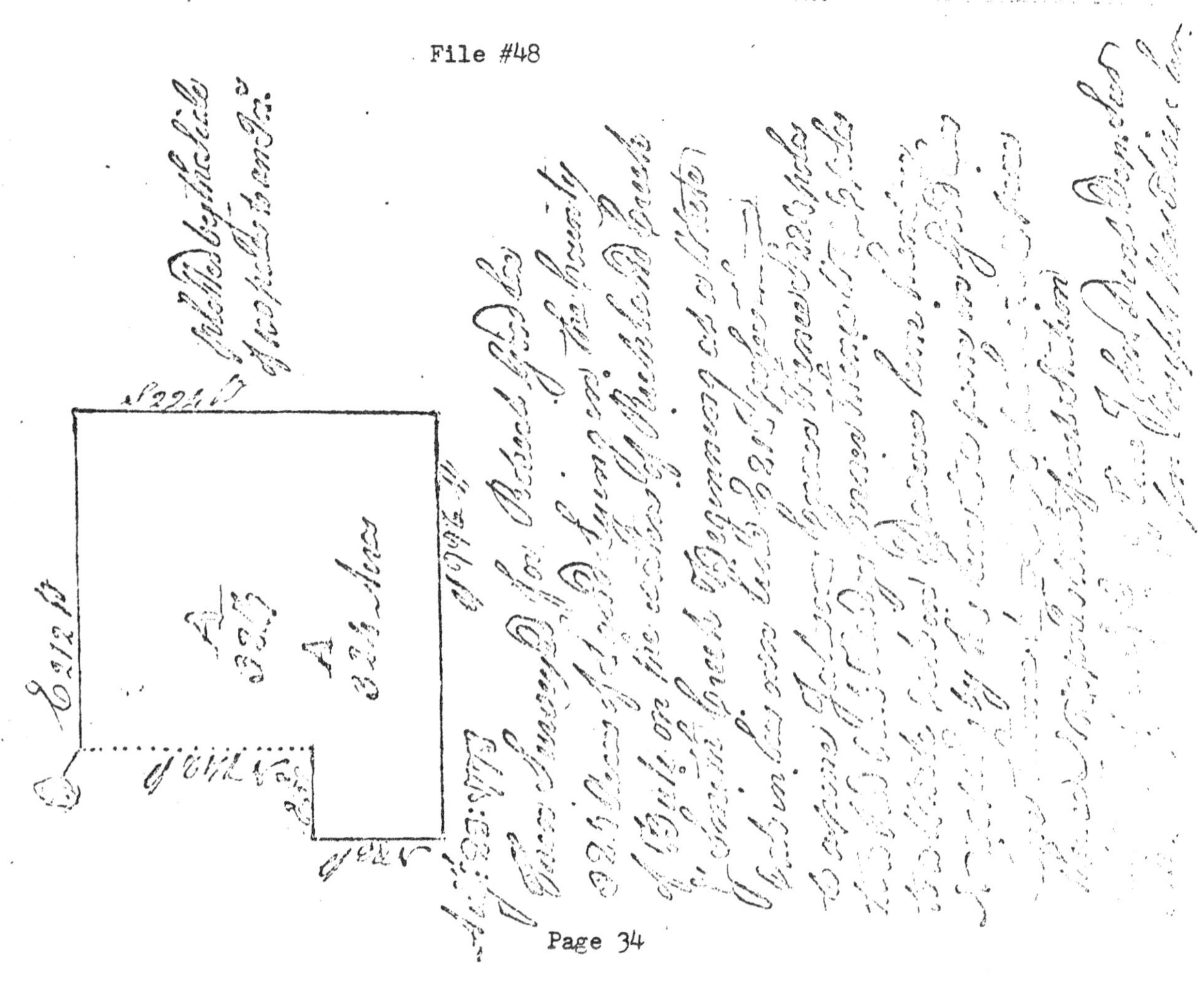

File #50

Laid Down by a scale of two Hundred pole to an Inch

August 26th 1778 Surveyd for Jno. Richards 361 acres of land according to the above plan lying in Bute County on the head of lyons Creek Beginning at a post oak in hawkins line at letter a thence S 4° E 117 poles by hawkins's line to a stake in Richards line at b thence by his line N° 88 E 236 poles Cross two small Branches of lions Creek to a Red oak at C thence N° 102 to a white O at D thence E 42 poles to a white oak at E thence N° 120 poles to a pine at f thence E 26 pole to a Black Jack at g thence N° 152 poles to a Red oak on the [illegible] side flat Rock Creek at h thence W° across flatrock 67 poles to a Black [illegible] in hawkins line at I thence by his line S° 153 poles to a white oak at k thence W° 125 pole to a post oak at l thence S° 115 pole to a hickory at m thence W° 132 to the first station for Jos. Hawkins Jur.

Solomon Bennett
Curtis Richards
Sw. Ch Carr's

by Wm Christmas D.S.

File #49

Laid Down By a scal of two Hundred Pole to an Inch

Surv. Octo 1st 1778 for Call Hill, 50 acres of Land according to the above Lying In Bute County Beginning at Jos Egertons Corner a Red oak at the Letter a thence N° 3 W° By his line 113 pole to a post oak In wilmot Egertons line at B thence By sd line S 88 W° 102 pole to 3 Black Jacks at C thence By Jno Egertons Corner S 3 E 109 pole to a Red oak Harris Corner at D thence By his line to first station

John Brown
Wilmot Egerton

Sworn Ch Carr. by Jos. Hawkins D.S.

Laid Down By a Scale of two Hundred Pole to an Inch

Surv^d^ octob^r^ 28th 1778 for Wm Phelps 320 acres of Land according to the above Plan lying In Burke County Beginning at a Red oak at the Letter A thence E 318 Pole to Glovers Corner a White oak at B thence By his line N° 80 pole to a Stake at C thence W^t^ 416 Pole to a popular Parsons Corner, line Continued 199 Pole to a White oak Parsons Corner In Nichols line at D thence By Nichols & Thorntons line S^o^ 246 Pole to a Black Jack thence to first Station

Abraham Childress

Ch^n^ Glover Sw^n^ Ch^n^ Cars

Wm Hawkins

File #51

File #52

Laid Down By a Scale of two hundred to an Inch

Surveyed Sept 3rd 1778 for Mathew Daniel 353 acres of Land according to the above Plan lying in Burke County on the S^o^ Side ... Branch Beginning at a post oak on ... line at the ... thence W^t^ 198 pole to Hawkins Corner thence by his line the same Course 216 pole to a white oak in ... at B thence N^o^ ...

File #53

Plotted By a scale of two hundred Pole to an Inch

Surveyed October 20th 1771 for Philemon Hawkins Sr 436 acres of Land agreeable to the annexed plan lying In Bute County on the waters of Tinches Creek Beginning at a Red oak In Hawkins line at the [illegible] thence his & Jones's Line [illegible] 326 hole a cross a Branch of sd Creek to a stake at B thence [illegible] 122 hole to Richards Corner line Continued 92 hole to a Red oak at C thence [illegible] 326 hole to a stake at D thence [illegible] to the first station

Daniel Ruff
&
Charles Avent } S C C

by J Hawkins S

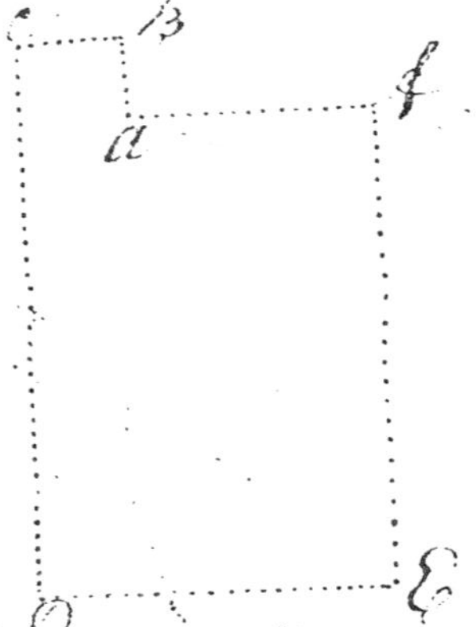

File #54

B

A

F

E

D

Laid Down By a Scale of two
Hundred Pole to an Inch

Surveyd August the 7th 1778 for
Joseph Hawkins 250 acres of land
according to the above Plan lying
In Bute County on the waters of
Lindseys Creek Beginning at a pine D
Reeveses Corner at the [illegible] thence By Hawkins
Line [illegible] pole to a white oak & hickory at B
thence E 70 pole to a white & Red oak at C thence
N [illegible] pole thro the wildcat pond to a hickory
& white oak at D thence [illegible] pole to two
Black Jacks at E thence [illegible] 366 pole along
Lindseys Creek to a Stake in hawkins line
at F thence By his line to first Station

Charles [illegible] & James [illegible] } Chain Bearers [illegible]

J. Hawkins

File #55

Laid down by a scale of two
Hundred po[les] to an Inch —
Surveyed April 12 1778 for —
Buchanan Dixon 200 acres of
Land according to the above plat
Lying in Burke County on both
sides of the Rock Creek Beginning
at Dixons New Corner on a Red oak at the —
[illegible] thence N° 57 W. 220 pole to a Red
oak at B thence [illegible] 175 pole to a white oak
In hawkins New line at C thence by s[ai]d line
N.° 65 pole to a Black Oak at D [illegible] Corner
thence by his line E 67 pole along the [illegible]
[illegible] to a Red oak on [illegible]
[illegible] 71 poles to a Black Oak at F thence to
[illegible] first Station —
James [illegible])

George Miller } [illegible]

[illegible] Chain Car[riers]

J. Hawkins S.

File #56

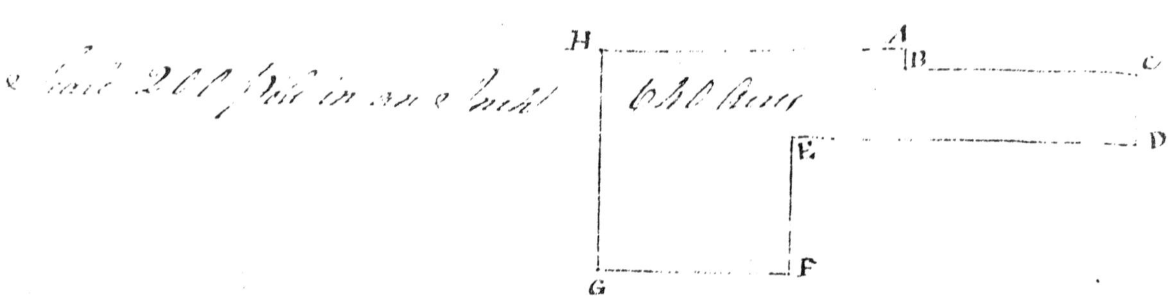

Sept. 18th 1778 I Surveyed for [illegible] the following Tract of Land lying [in] Burke County on the waters of [illegible] Creek Containing 640 Acres Beginning at a [illegible] Oak [illegible] Corner thence [illegible] along the line [illegible] to a [illegible] Oak [illegible] thence [illegible] along the line 206 [illegible] Corner thence along the line 86 [illegible] to a [illegible] Corner thence [illegible] along the line 434 [illegible] Corner thence [illegible] along the line [illegible] to a [illegible] Oak in the line thence [illegible] 228 [illegible] Corner thence [illegible] along the line 164 [illegible] Corner [illegible] 260 [illegible] Oak [illegible] to the Beginning [illegible]

Joseph [illegible]

John [illegible]
A[illegible] } Ch. Car.

[illegible] 1778 then Surveyed for Charles Durnal 592 acres of Land in Burk County lying on waters of Cedar Creek Beginning at Rollands Corner [illegible] thence S 236 poles to a pine thence N 107 poles to a pine Anderson's Corner thence E 146 poles to a Lightwood Knot thence N 40 p to a White Oak thence E 120 p. to a White Oak on Perrys line thence S 206 p. to a Hickory thence E 140 poles to Hickory thence S poles to a Spanish Oak thence W 204 poles to a White Oak thence to the first station

Moses Durnal } Chain
Jesse Roland Junr. } Carriers

Pr. me John Dent Dep. Survr.
for Joseph Hawkins Surveyor

File #57

File #58

Scale 100 poles in an Inch.

July 15th 1778 Surveyed for John Simmonds the following Tract of land lying in Burk County on the Branches of the Cypress Containing 300 Acres Beginning at a Spanish Oak Dinsons Corr. Thence Et. Along his line 206 p to a White Oak Thence So. 233 P. to a pine Thence Et. 17 P to a May pole his own Corner Thence No. Along his line 354 Pole to a Red Oak in his line Thence W. 60 P to a Cor. Thence No. Along Elovs line 104 Pc. to a Black Jack Thence W 154 P to a Red Oak & B Jack Thence to the first Station

Joseph Hawkins

Jno. Helms } Ch. Carrs.
Jas. Barrow }

Feb. 17th 1778 Then Surveyed for Henry Hill Junr 293 Acres of Land lying in Wake County on the South side of Tar River Beginning at [illegible] Bakers own Corner thence South 210 po. to a White oak thence E 50 po. to a [illegible] pine Bakers Corner thence N 120 po. to a White oak Bakers Corner thence N 78 po. to a Black Jack Bakers Corner thence W 158 po. to a W Oak Rolands Corner thence N 78 p to a spanish Oak [illegible] thence E 234 po. to a Hickory [illegible] Murphery Corner thence [illegible] E 132 po. to a pine thence S 130 po. to a pine thence to the Beginning

Demsey Bunyard } Chain
Joshua Jones } Carriers

[illegible] John [illegible]
for Joseph [illegible]

Laid Down By a Scale of two Hundred to an Inch

Surv.d August 5th 1778 for John Ahert 342 acres of land according to the above Plan Lying in Bute County on Rocky Creek & andersons Swamp Beginning at a pine Ballards Corner at the Letter a thence E.t 109 to Walkers Corner a post oak at B thence By his Line N.o 82 pole to the old Court House Road thence along the s.d Walkers & Cothorns line the same Course 177 pole to a pine In Cothorns Line at C thence By W.ms line W.t 60 pole to a Black Oake at D thence By W.ms line N.o 46 pole to a pine On Linseys line at E thence By his line W.t 77 pole to Cothorns Corner a hickory Bush at f thence By his Line S.o 350 pole to his Corner a post oak ~~thence~~ at G thence By s.d line W.t 121 pole a Cross a Branch of andersons Swamp to two Black Oaks at H thence S.o 35 E.t 152 pole to a post oak at I Such on the N.o side the old Road thence to the first Station

Tho.s Cothorn } Sw Ch Car.s
Ja.s Walker }

by [illegible] Surv.r

File #61

Scale 200 poles in an Inch

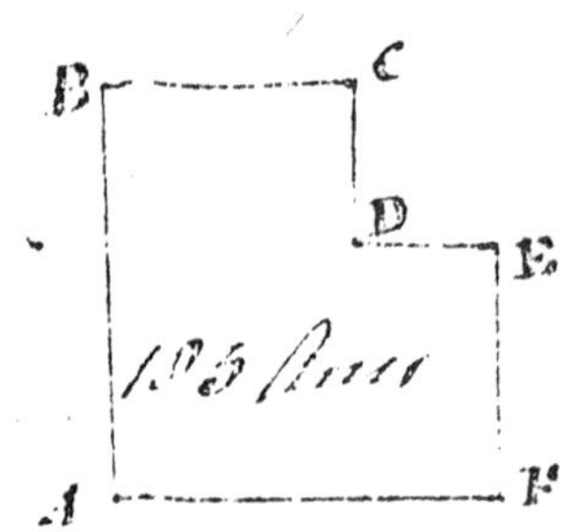

July 3 1770 Surveyed for Wm. [illegible] the following Tract of Land lying in [illegible] County on the fork of [illegible] Beginning at [illegible] Corner [illegible] Thence [illegible] along [illegible] 232 po. to a [illegible] Oak [illegible] Corner Thence [illegible] 156 po. to a Spanish Oak in [illegible] Thence [illegible] along [illegible] line 100 po. to a [illegible] Corner Thence [illegible] along his line 86 po. [illegible] Oak [illegible] Thence [illegible] [illegible] line 132 po. to a [illegible] Oak. Thence to the first Station Including 183 Acres

Joseph Hawkins

Geo: Smith }
John Ratcliff } Ch. C.

Sub. 200 [illegible]

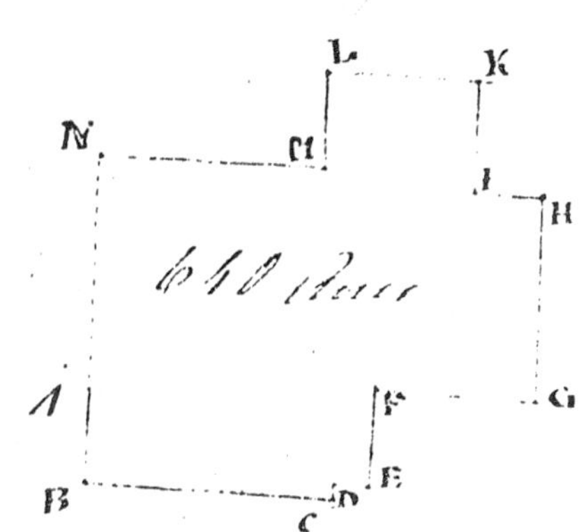

Sepr 1. 1778 Surveyed for Ralph [illegible] the following Tract of Land lying in [illegible] County Containing 640 Acres Beginning at a [illegible] thence [illegible] po. to a [illegible] thence [illegible] po. to a [illegible] thence [illegible] po. [illegible] thence [illegible] po. to a [illegible] thence [illegible] po. [illegible] thence [illegible] po. to a [illegible] thence [illegible] po. to [illegible] thence [illegible] to the first station

Wm [illegible] } Ch. Carrs
Thos [illegible]

Joseph [illegible] Sur.

... by a scale of two hundred to an Inch

Surv'd Nov'r 3rd 1778 for Joseph [illegible] Williams 80 acres of land according to the above Plan lying in Burke County on both sides Lyons Creek Beginning at a Red oak on [illegible] old line thence W 123 Pole to a post oak at B thence N 320 pole across Lyons Creek to a [illegible] Stump on a Branch of s'd Creek at C thence E 20[illegible] pole to a white oak at D thence across Lyons Creek to first Station

[illegible]

George Parker [illegible] by W. Hawkins Dep.

File #63

File #65

Laid Down By a scale of two Hundred pole to an Inch

Surveyed Octob'r 2nd 1778 for henry felts 164 acres of land according to the above Plan lying in Burke County on the waters of hawtree Beginning at a [illegible] Downeys Corner at the letter A thence N by [illegible] & his own 200 pole to a pine on [illegible] line on a Branch of hawtree at B thence by [illegible] line E 103 pole to a [illegible] on a Branch of hawtree at C on [illegible] line thence S by his [illegible] line 200 pole to [illegible] Corner a pine on Downeys line at D thence by Downeys line to first Station

Henry [illegible]

Ephraim [illegible] by W. Hawkins Dep.

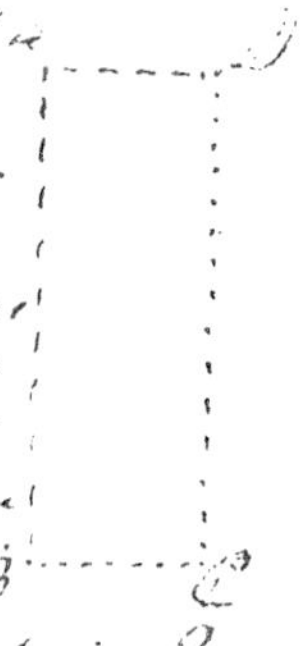

Laid Down By a Scale of
two Hundred Pole to an Inch

Surv.d August 1st 1778 for
Wm Darnall 640 acres of land
according to the above Plan —
Lying in Bute County on the
Waters of Shocco Swamp
Creek Beginning at Bafors
Corner a Red oak at the Letter A thence By his Sd
& Bennetts line N 80 E 300 Pole to Summers
Corner a white oak at B thence By his line N [illegible]
E 300 Pole to Summers Corner on Willemores line
at C thence By Willemores line S 80 W 40 pole
to a hickory on the S. Side Shocco at D thence up
the Various Courses to the head at E thence W.
50 Pole to a Red oak Wm Corner at F thence By
his Sd line S 10 W 300 to a Red oak Kings line at G
thence N 80 W [illegible] Pole to a Red oak a fork Hawkins
Rode at H thence E 155 Pole to a Red oak at A
Thence to first Station

Stephen Beckham
&
Jno Beckham Sworn Carr.

W. Hawkins S.

[illegible] Warrant of [illegible] to an Entry
[illegible] 1779 — Surveyed for Michael Collins
852 acres of land agreeable to the Comand [illegible]
Plan Lying in Bute County Between [illegible] B
Creek & [illegible] Beginning at Davis Corner
[illegible] at the [illegible] thence by his line N°
S 40 W 210 pole to a [illegible] oak thence by [illegible]
line W 160 pole to Wilson Corner a Red oak [illegible]
by his line N 130 Pole to Wilson Corner [illegible]
68 pole to a Red oak thence N° [illegible] Collins [illegible]
126 pole to a Red oak thence N 90 pole to a [illegible]
Creek 148 pole to Collins Corner by his line [illegible]
Corner 320 pole to Red bud Creek thence down the
Creek [illegible] 150 pole to William [illegible]
thence by his line N 228 to the first station

Peter [illegible] } [illegible] Car[illegible] } By [illegible] Coleman
Wm [illegible]

Surveyd August 21st 1778 for Benjamin Kimbell 600 acres of land accordeing to this plan lying in Rutherford County Beginning at a white oak in Sugar Jones line at a thence by his line N° 2 W 450 poles to a pine at b thence N° 88 E 176 pole to hawkins Corner spanish oak C thence by his line N° 2 W 30 pole to a white oak at a D thence S° 88 E 164 pole to a white oak E thence N° 2 W 55 pole to a pine at f thence S 87 W 261 pole crosses the turkill branch by McLemore path to a Red oak Hawkins Corner in Clements line at g thence by his line S° 2 W 63 pole to his corner a post oak at h thence S 86 W 68 pole to Summers Corner In Clements line at I thence by Summers line S 3 W 130 pole to a post oak at K thence along Summers & Kimbells line N° 88 E 212 pole across the Buzzard Branch to Kimbells Corner a pine at l thence by his line S 2 E thro his Dwelling house 361 pole to a stake in Jones line at m thence to first station

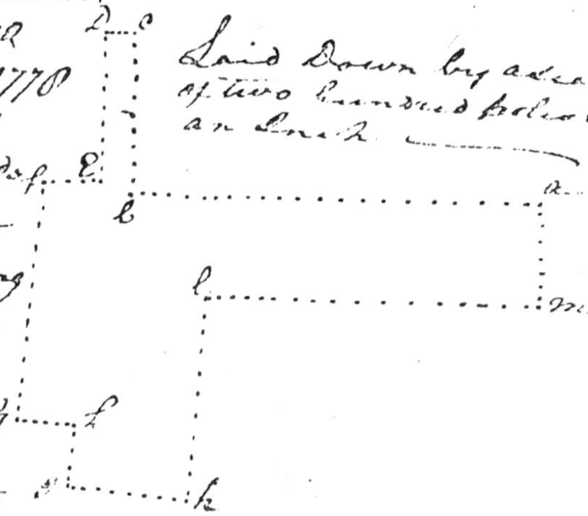

Laid Down by a scale of two hundred poles to an Inch

David Kimbell
&
Benjamin Kimbell
Sw, Ch, Car.

for Jo. Hawkins Survr
by Wm Christmas D S

File #68

Laid Down By a scale of two Hundred pole to an Inch

Surveyed August 27th 1770 for Zachariah Dixon 650 acres of land according to the above plan lying in Burk County on [illegible] Side [illegible] Creek Beginning at a [illegible] corner in Younges line at a pine at [illegible] thence By Younges & common line N° 2 W[t] 274 [illegible] pole [illegible] flat Rock to a pine [illegible] at [illegible] thence N [illegible] W[t] 88 pole to a Red oak [illegible] thence N 40 W[t] 114 pole along flat Rock Creek to a Black Oak in Richardsons [illegible] at D thence By [illegible] line [illegible] pole to a Black Jack [illegible] thence W[t] 80 pole to a pine at F thence N [illegible] pole [illegible] at G thence E 96 pole to a pine at [illegible] thence [illegible] Black Jack at [illegible] thence N 23 E 100 pole to a Black Oak at K thence N 80 pole to a Red oak at [illegible] line thence by his line to the first Station

George Willis }
Tho[s] Cannon } Sw[n] Ch Carr[s] by [illegible]

[illegible]

File #69

Laid Down By a Scal of
Two hundred fifty to an Inch

Surv^d August 17th 1779 for
Andrew Raley 296 acres of
Land according to the above Plan lying
In Burke County on Lyons Creek Beg^g
at hills Corner a Red oak at the Letter A
thence By his line S^o 76 Pole to a pine
Raleys Corner at B thence By his line
W^t 116 Pole to a white oak Raleys Corner at C thence
By his line N° 92 Pole to a pine at D thence W^t
116 Pole to a Red oak at E thence By Raleys line
N° 178 Pol to Raleys Corner In Walkers line a
Black Jack at F thence By Walkers Line E
119 Pole to his Corner a white oak at G thence
By his line N° 134 Pole R^ds Corner a pine at H
thence E By R^ds line 80 Pole to a hickory In W^ms
Line at I thence By W^ms line S^o 209 Pole
to W^ms Corner a white oak at K thence By his
line E 326 Pole to a pine at L thence By S line
S^o 154 Pole to a pine at M thence W^t 99 Pole
to two Red oaks In hills Line at N thence By
his line N° 100 Pole to a Stake at O thence
By hills line to first Station

Sworn
Wm Richards
&
Fedrick Roling } Surv^d by Wm Christmas Dep^y
for Joseph [illegible] S

File #70

Plotted By a Scale of two Hundred
Poles to an Inch

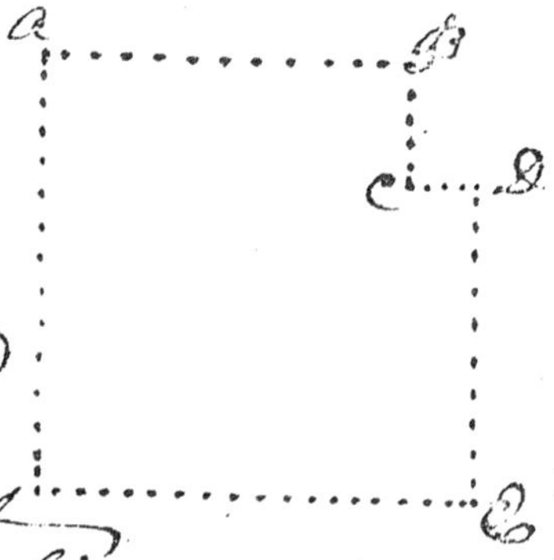

Surveyed Octob.r the 5th 1771 for
Charles artlee 240 acres of Land
agreeable to the annexed Plan Lying
In Bute County on the Waters of Linches Creek
Beginning at a pine Jones Corner In hawkins
line on the West side S.d Creek at the Little a thence by
Jones line W.t 272 Pole to a Red oak thence By
hikes line N.o 92 Pole to a Dead White oak thence
By his line W.t 52 Pole to haggards Corner a hickory
thence By haggards line N.o 243 pole to a hickory
thence E.t 323 Pole to a Stake On Hawkins line
thence By his line S.t across Linches Creek to first
Station

Jones Weldon
James Merritt SCC   By Ph Hawkins S

A B C D E

File #71

Scale 200 poles in an Inch

432 Acres

G H E F B A D C

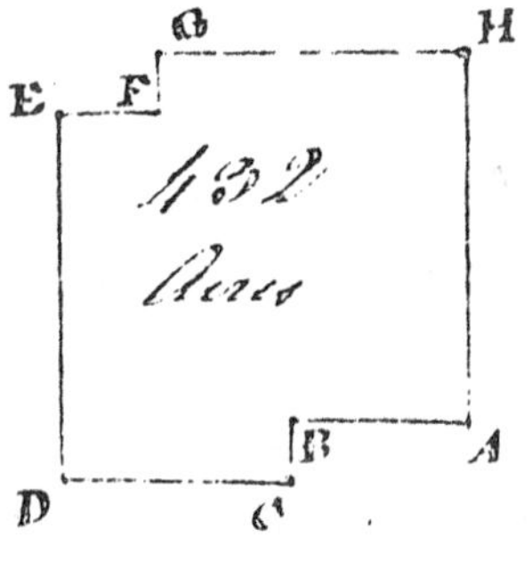

Aug^st 31. 1738 Surveyed for Wm. [illegible] the
above Tract of Land in Kent County Lying
on the N. W. Side of Cedar Creek Containing 432
Acres Beg. at a White Oak in [illegible] thence
W. 120 p. to a White Oak thence [illegible] 142 p. [illegible]
White Oak thence N. 60 p. to [illegible] line
thence N. along his line 250 p. to a White Oak [illegible]
thence [illegible] along his line 180 p. to a [illegible] thence [illegible]
to a [illegible] Oak [illegible] thence [illegible] along his line 200 p. to [illegible]
[illegible] line thence to the first Station

Wm. Bridges }
Jos. Robinson } Ch. B.

Joseph [illegible]

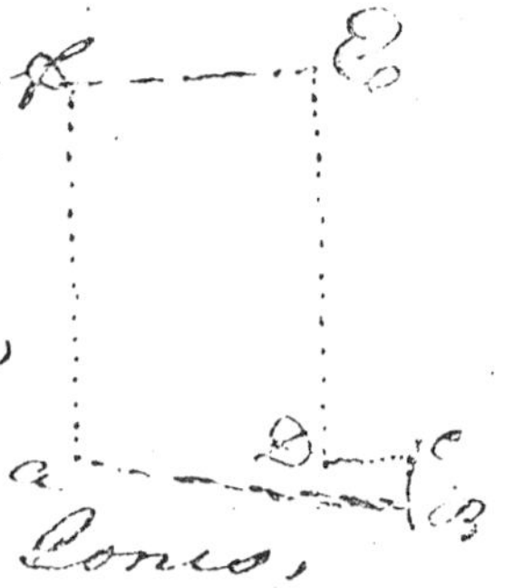

Laid Down By a scale of two hundred Pole to an Inch

Surveyed Octo 27th 1778 for John May 300 Acres of land according to the above Plan Lying In Burke County on the waters of Lower Creek of Six Pound Beginning at a white oak Jones's Corner at the Little ... Creek on the N Side a Branch of ... Creek a Six Pound thence By Jones's line N 10 E 200 Pole to a white oak In a Branch of Six Pound at D thence up Sd Branch W 49 Pole to a maple at E thence By Nichols line S 32 Pole to a white oak his Corner at B thence By his S line W 220 Pole to a white O line Continued 300 Pole to a white at C thence S 162 Pole across a Branch of paw tree to a Red oak at F Thence to first Station.

Jno Elliot

Charles Weekly Sw Ch Car

J. Hutchins Co. Sur.

File #74

Laid down By a scale of two Hundred Pole to an Inch
Surveyed Sept 30th 1772 for Thomas Cook 300 acres of
Land according to the above Lying in Bute County on the
waters of [illegible] on Both sides the Church Road Beginning
at Jones's corner a white oak at the [illegible] thence By his
line N 83 E [illegible] pole along the sd Road to a stump in the [illegible]
thence By [illegible] line N [illegible] pole along the sd Road [illegible]
the Church Door to a stake [illegible] at C thence N
21 Pole to a white [illegible] Corner at D thence N 87 E 41 pole
to [illegible] corner a [illegible] at E thence By his line to the
first station

[illegible] Jones
Robt Jones Chain Carriers   Jn Washington Surv

File #73

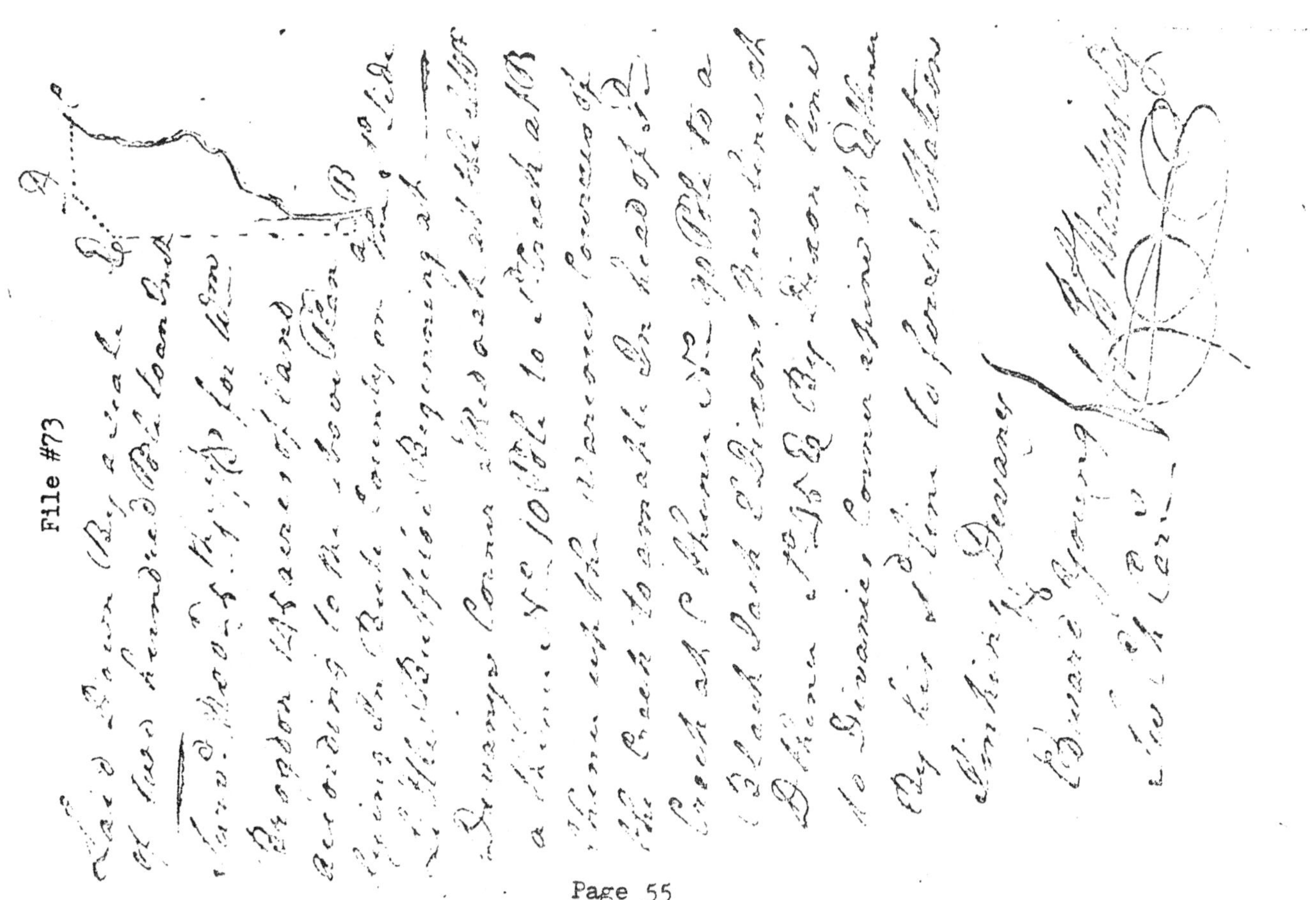

Laid down by a Scale of two
[illegible] to an Inch

Surveyed Sept 23rd 1773 for
Wm St John [illegible] of land
according to the above Plan
lying in [illegible] County on
the waters of [illegible] Creek Beginning at Jordans
Corner [illegible] the [illegible] thence E 190 Pole
to a pine [illegible] line at B thence By
[illegible] line [illegible] Pole to a stake at C thence E
178 Pole [illegible] Branch of [illegible] Creek to
a Red oak in [illegible] line at D thence
S By [illegible] line [illegible] Pole to a Red oak at E thence
W 120 pole to a black Oak at f thence N 60
Pole to a Black Oak at g thence W 100 Pole
[illegible] to a Red oak at H thence
N 100 Pole to a Red oak at I thence W 148 pole
to a pine in Jordans line [illegible] thence
By [illegible] line to first Station

Thos Thorn
[illegible] Thorn } [illegible]

Jos Hawkins

File #76

Sept 9th 1777 } N 200 poles to an Ash
then Surveyed for John Wright 640
Acres of Land lying in the County
of Bute on the Waters of Crooked Creek
Beginning at a Hickory Bryan Terrels
line thence S 168 Wt to a pine Terrels Corner
thence E 42 poles along sd Terrel Line to a White Oak thence
S 86 poles to a White Oak thence E 322 poles to a pine thence N 90
poles along sd Parsons line to White Oak thence E 62 poles
to a pine thence N 157 poles to a pine thence W 426 poles to the first
Station

Edward Freeman } Chain
Wm Freeman } Carriers } Wm John Dent Dept Survr
for Joseph Hawkins Sur

File #79

N 200 poles

October 9th 1778 Surveyed for Isbell 98 Acres of Land
In Bute County Beginning at 3 Corner pines on the
Head of Little Creek thence E 120 Poles to a pine thence S 110
Poles to a Spanish Oak on said Creek thence S 29 W 27
to the first Station per Me John Dent DS

Isbl Edward } Chain Carriers for Joseph Hawkins S
Charles Blac }

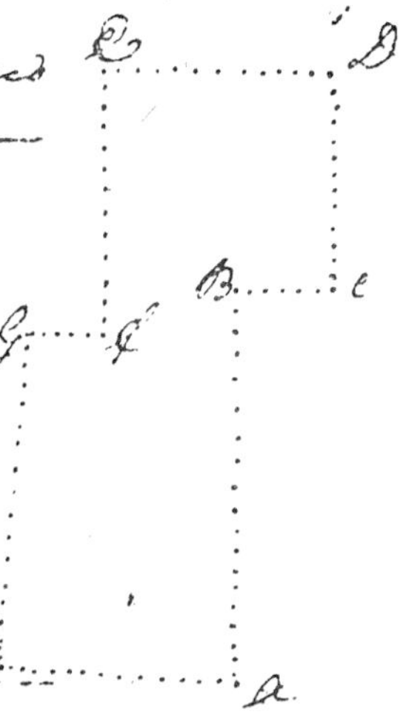

File #77

Laid Down By a scale of two Hundred
Pole to an Inch ———

E . . . . . . D

B C

G

A

Surveyed August 8th 1778 for Adkin
McLemore 500 acres of Land according
to the above Plan lying In Burke
County on the waters of fishing
Creek Beginning at a Red oak
at the letter A thence By Wm's line
N° 4 W 323 Pole to his Corner a post
oak at B thence N° 85 E 84 Pole to Browns Corner
In Wm's line a Red oak at C thence N° 4 W 178
Pole to Duties line a stake at D thence By
Duties line S° 89 W 185 Pole to Barchits Corner
a hickory at E thence By his line S° 8 E 213 Pole
to Barchits Corner a pine at F thence By his line
S° 86 W 60 Pole to a post oak at G thence S°
67 Pole to a Black oak at H thence East across
a Branch of fishing Creek to first Station

Wm Dernold
Jn° Buckham
Sw. Ch. Carr.

Jn° Dickins Sur
by Wm Christmas D.S.

File #78

Scale 200 po. to an Inch

E F G H
640
D C B A I

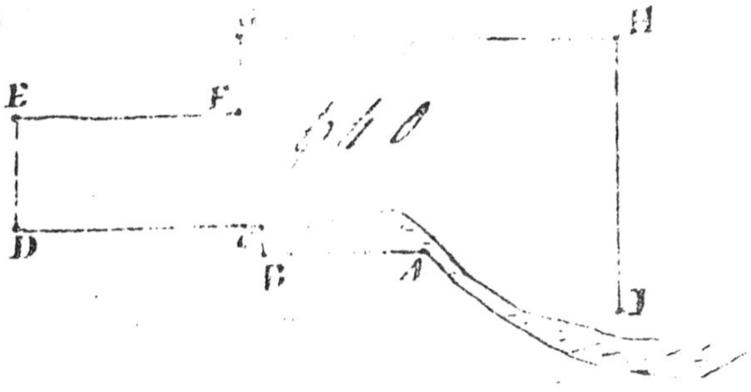

July 9. 1778 Surveyed for Wm. Dixon the following Tract of Land lying in Burke County on Stark's Cre. Beginning at a Poplar Hickory Cor. thence W. 152 po. to a Spanish Oak thence N. 10 po. to a [illegible] & Black Jack [illegible] Supposed [illegible] Cor. Thence W. along his line 250 po. to a Hickory & [illegible] Simmons Cor. Thence N. along his line thro' his field 100 po. to a Spanish Oak Cor. Thence E. along his line 205 po. to a Red Oak his Cor. Thence N. along his line 68 po. to a Black Jack in his line Thence E. 400 po. to a White Oak in his line Thence S. along his line 235 po. to a White Oak in Stark's Cre. Thence up Stark's Cre. to the first Station Including 640 Acres.

Joseph Hawkins Sur.

John Carr }
John Simmons } Ch. Car.

File #80

[illegible]

B C

640 Acres

D
E

A F

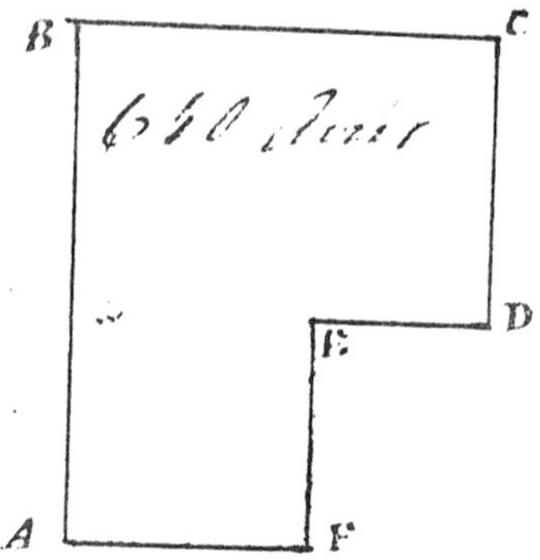

July 13th 1779 Surveyed for Edmd. Duncan the following Tract of Land lying in Burke County joining [illegible] containing 640 Acres Beginning at a [illegible] Duncans [illegible] in Cane [illegible] [illegible] 80 [illegible] 260 [illegible] 602 [illegible] 216 [illegible] to a [illegible] Duncans line [illegible] 126 [illegible] 190 [illegible] to the Beginning [illegible]

Joseph [illegible]

[illegible] } Ch. Carr.
Joshua Coggin }

Scale 200 poles an Inch.

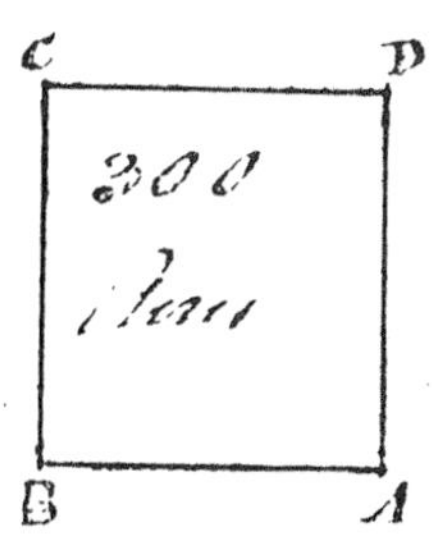

July 16th 1778 Surveyed for Wm. [illegible] the following Tract of Land in [illegible] County lying on the Branches of Little [illegible] Containing 300 Acres Beginning at a pine in [illegible] line on a Branch of the [illegible] Thence West along his line 200 po. to a [illegible] Cor. Thence N. along his line 200 po. to a [illegible] in [illegible] line Thence E. 200 po. to a White Oak Thence to the first station.

John [illegible]
Edmd. [illegible] } C. Crs.

Joseph [illegible]

File #82

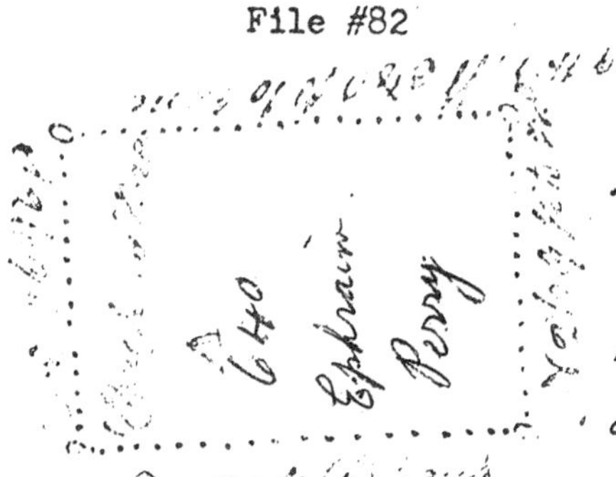

Aug. 23 1778

Then Surveyed for Ephra im Perry 640 Acres of Land lying in Bute County on Buckers Branch Beginning at Nathaniel Perry Corner White Oak thence W. 380 po. to a pine on Buckers Branch thence S 269 poles to a Black Jack thence E 380 poles to a Black Jack thence N 269 poles to ye Beginning

Thos. Arnold Junr. } Chane Carriers
Joseph Wright }

} Pr me John Dent Dp Surr
for. Joseph Hawkins S.

640 Ephraim Perry

File #83

October the 19th 1778 Surveyed for James Morris 417 Acres of Land Laying in Bute County Beginning at Goodlou Corner a pine on the waters of [illegible] Creek [illegible] 200 poles to an [illegible] Red Oak thence N 73 E 27 Poles to a white oak thence S 178 Poles to a white oak thence E 136 Poles to a white Oak thence N 264 to a black Jack thence E 3[illegible] Poles to a Pine thence N 23[illegible] Poles to a black [illegible] thence W 30 Poles to a [illegible] thence [illegible] W 410 Poles to the first Station Pr me John Dent D.S.

Robert [illegible] } Chain Carriers for. Joseph Hawkins S.
Isaac Winston }

417

File #84

Scale 200 Poles in an Inch

E D C B
F G
334 Acres
H A

Sept. 10. 1770 Surveyed for John Thomas the following Tract of Land lying in Bute County on the waters of [illegible] Creek on the [illegible] side of [illegible] the Spring Branch Beginning at a Black Jack Thomas [illegible] in [illegible] line thence [illegible] along his line 156 po. to a W. Oak Glebe Cor. thence W. along Glebe line 196 po. to a pine Glebe Cor. [illegible] Cor. 60 po. to a Black Jack in the road thence N. 20 W. [illegible] Jack in the road thence West 90 po. to a pine thence S. 80 po. to a W. Oak thence West 22 po. to a [illegible] Richmond's Cor. thence S. along his line 96 po. to a Red Oak [illegible] Cor. thence to the first Station.

Joseph [illegible]

Rich. [illegible] } Ch. Carr.
John Guinn }

File #85

August 25th 1772 I Surveyd for Thos Arendel 640 Acres of Land Lying in Bute County on Waters of Crooked Creek Beginning at Perrys Corner thence E 80 Poles to Perrys Corner thence N 200 Poles to a white oak thence West 256 Poles to a white oak thence S 34 Poles to a hickory thence W 80 Poles to a white oak thence S 26 Poles to a red oak thence E 256 Poles to a white oak thence N 160 to the first station

Scale 200 poles to an inch

640

E 80

N 160

E 256

John Dent
Thos Arendel Junr } Chain Carriers pr. Joseph Hawkins Sur.
Joseph Knight

File #86

Laid Down by a scal of two hundred to an Inch

Surveyd April 14th 1772 for Richard Walker [illegible] acres of land according to the above Plan lying in Bute County On [illegible] Mill Creek Beginning at letter A on the N side of the Creek on [illegible] line thence By the line N 91 [illegible] to [illegible] Corner a hickory at letter B thence by the line [illegible] to the Creek at C thence Down the various courses to the first station

Robert Walker
Wm [illegible] } Ch. Carr.

Jos. Hawkins

File #87

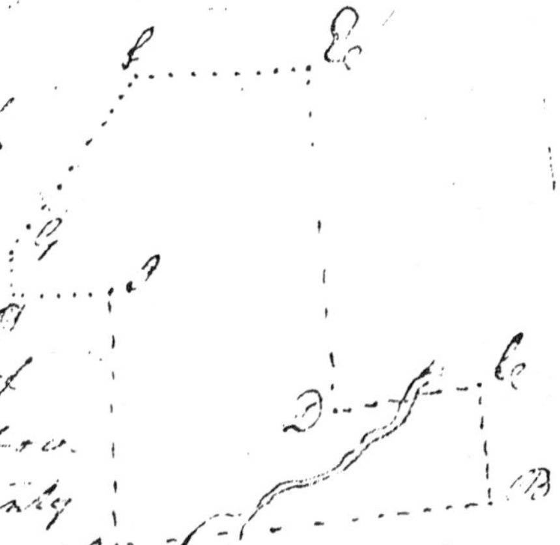

Laid Down by a scale of
One hundred pole to an
Inch

Surveyed August [illegible] 1770
for
Willm Richards 174 acres of
Land according to the above
Plan lying in Bute County
on both sides Lyons Creek
Beginning in Wm Richards line on a white
[illegible] at A thence by his line S 1 E 176 pole
to a pine at B thence E 80 pole to a hickory on
Williams [illegible] at C thence by his line N 7
E 71 pole along Lyons Creek to a Dead maple
Wm Corner at D thence by sd line N 00 E
46 pole to a Red oak at E thence N 00 pole
[illegible] Black oak at F thence N 53 Wt 100 pole
to a Black Jack at G thence Wt 20 pole to
to a white oak at H thence [illegible] 85 pole to a pine
at I thence to the first Sta[illegible]

Robert Walker } Chain Carriers
Curtis Richards }

Wm Christmas D S
for Joseph [illegible]

File #88

Laid Down By a scal of One hundred pole to an Inch Surveyd august 19th 1778 for William Brock 400 acres of Land according to the annexed plan lying in Burke County on the N. side Sandy Creek Beginning at a popular B on the North side of the creek on Hawkins line at the Little Branch thence Down the Various Courses of the Creek to a white Oak fortner line Inch Below the Rode at D thence By fortners & Christmas line N° 40 190 pole to a pine at C thence By Christmas line S° 86 E 104 pole along the Bounder to a white oak at E thence N° 122 pole to a post oak at E thence W. 96 pole to a Redoak & post oak at f thence by hawkins line S° 157 pole to a Black Oak at G thence to the first station

Griffen Dickerson } by [illegible]
Moses Fortner
Sulch Can[illegible]

W Hawkins S.

File #89

Laid Down By a scale of two hundred to an Inch

Sept 11th 1778 Surveyed James Ransom 100 acres of land according to the above Plan lying in Bute County Beginning at Masons Corner three Redoaks at the letter A thence By Masons line S° 85 Wt 27/3 pole to a post oak at B thence N° 50 pole to a Red oak in Ransoms line at C thence By his line N° 85 E 27/3 pole to a post oak allens Corner at D thence to first Station

Lewis Parham
Jeffrey Mustan
Ch. Carr. } by J. Hawkins

Laid Down By a scale of two Hundred pole to an Inch

Surveyed Sept 12th 1778 for John Hawkins Junr 30 acres of land according to the above Plan lying in Bute County near Sandy Creek Beginning at Tabbs Corner a pine at the letter A thence By his line So 2° E 100 pole to a white oak at B thence N° 83 E 60 pole to [illegible] Corner a white oak at C thence by his line N° 33 Wt 110 pole to [illegible] in [illegible] line at D thence Wt to first Station

Sol. Eaton
[illegible]
Chain Carr. } [illegible]

J. Hawkins

File #90

File #91

Sc. 200 p[illegible] to an Inch

[illegible] 16th 1778 [illegible] for James [illegible] 110 acres of land lying in the County of Bute on the Waters of the [illegible] swamp on [illegible] side of [illegible] Beginning at a black Jack thence [illegible] 152 poles to a pine thence [illegible] 170 poles to [illegible] Branch thence [illegible] poles to [illegible] line to a [illegible] thence [illegible] to a [illegible] thence [illegible] to a [illegible] thence to the Beginning

John [illegible]
[illegible]
[illegible]

[illegible] John [illegible]
for
[illegible] Hawkins

File #92

Said Plan By scale of two Hundred pole to an Inch

Surveyed August 12th 1778 for Bailey Fleming 246 acres of land according to the above plan lying in Bute County on the Branches of Fishing Creek [illegible] Andersons Swamp Beginning at Barkers Corner a post oak [illegible] thence by Boundary line [illegible] 87d E 234 poles to a post oak [illegible] thence [illegible] 2d E 20 poles to a Red Oak In the [illegible] line [illegible] thence by the [illegible] line [illegible] 77d E 78 pole to Ballards Corner a pine at E thence by his line [illegible] 2d [illegible] 264 poles to his Corner a pine at F thence by [illegible] line [illegible] 70d [illegible] 57 poles to a post oak on the [illegible] side the old Court House Road at G thence [illegible] 35 [illegible] 152 poles to a Black Oak in [illegible] line at H thence by his line [illegible] 88d [illegible] 58 poles to [illegible] Corner a Red Oak at I thence by [illegible] line [illegible] 3d E 190 pole to a pine at K thence by a Conventable line [illegible] 81 [illegible] 102 pole to a post oak at L thence [illegible] 30 [illegible] 94 poles to a Red oak at [illegible] thence to the first station

Joseph [illegible]
Jas. Bailey
[illegible]

[illegible]
[illegible] Hawkins

File #93

Augt 3 1778 [illegible] 200 poles to one in Green surveyed for Linnon Lanceford 300 Acres of Land Lying in Bute County on the waters of Crooked Creek Beginning at Thos Arnold Corner White Oak thence S 80 poles to a Hickory thence N 54 poles to a White Oak thence E 52 po to Youngs Corner pine thence N 28 poles to a pine Thos [illegible] Corner thence W 128 poles to a stone Joseph Bridges Corner thence N [illegible] poles to a White Oak Osborn Jeffreys [illegible] Corner thence [illegible] W 40 po to Jeffreys Corner Hickory thence S 245 poles to a pine thence E 56 poles to a thence S 62 poles to ye Beginning

John Green } Chain
John Winter } Carrier

{ p me John Dickinson [illegible]
for Joseph [illegible]

Decemb.r 5th 1778

Then Surveyed for Osborn Jeffreys 640 Acres of Land Lying in Bute County on both Sides of Crooked Creek Joining his own lines and Lunsum Lunsfords Thos. Bridges & Wm. Jeffreys Bounds Beginning at his own Corner Red Oak Northerly of Crooked Creek thence N 90 poles to a black Oak in Thos. Bridges bounds thence by ye Dividing lines E 100 poles to a pine on ye South Side of ye sd. Creek thence up ye sd. Creek W 54 poles to a pine on ye North Side of the sd. Creek thence S 110 poles to a black Oak thence E 60 poles to a pine thence by ye agreed bounds of Wm. Jeffreys S 120 poles to a pine thence E 188 poles to three black and two White Oaks Saplins thence S 200 poles to a Red & White Oak thence E 174 poles to a pine thence S 43 poles to a black Oak thence E 216 poles to a Spanish Oak on a small Run thence N 200 poles to a black Oak in Lenom Lunsfords line thence by the sd. Lunsford and his own old line W 330 poles to his Corner White Oak thence by a Nother of ye sd. Osborns lines N 183 poles to three White Oaks Saplins thence by a nother of his old lines W 110 poles to his Corner Spanish Oak thence N 117 poles to ye first Station

Paul Jeffreys } Chain
Benj. May } Carriers

Pr. me John Dent D. S
for Robt. Goodloe S

File #95

Laid Down by a Scale of two hundred poles in an Inch

Survey^d August 26th 1770 for Lucy McGuffge 129 acres of Land according to the above plan lying in Bute County Beginning at a White oak Jno Richardson's Corner on Washams line at the letter a thence by his line N° 87 W^t 132 to a stake at b on Someys line thence by his line S 3 W^t 153 poles to a hickrey at c thence N 88 E 27 pole to a post oak at d thence along Jones's line S 2 E 104 pole to a Spanish oak e Denmans Corner thence by his line E 71 pole to a hickrey at f Bennetts Corner thence along his & Richardson's line to the first Station

Solomon Bennett &
Curtis Richards
Sw^n Ch^n Car^s

Jo^s Montfort Esqr Sur^r
by Wm Christmas Dep^y

File #96

[illegible]

File #97

Sept. 5 1778

Then Surveyed for John Robin[illegible] 78 Acres of Land on the North Side of Cedar Creek Beginning [illegible] White Oak [illegible] Corner [illegible] N 25 poles to a White Oak [illegible] to Ridge [illegible] Corner thence N [illegible] poles to a [illegible] 200 poles [illegible] Oak [illegible] Corner thence [illegible] to the first Station [illegible]

James Murphey
[illegible] Chain [illegible]

[illegible] John [illegible] Deputy
for Joseph [illegible] Surv.

200 poles to a [illegible]

78

File #99

Laid Down By a Scale of two Hundred Pole to an Inch

Survey'd Nov. 3rd 1778 for George Lovell 640 Acres of Land according to the above Plan Lying In Bute County on Both Sides Lyons Creek Beginning at a white oak at the letter A thence E 105 Pole to a pine at B thence N 105 Pole to Wootons Corner a pine at C thence E 184 Pole to a White oak and Hickory Corner at D thence By his line S 393 Pole a Cross Lyons Creek to Wms Corner a pine at E thence W 193 Pole a Cross Several Small Branches of sd Creek to a pine Ralys Corner at F thence N 150 Pole to a pine at G thence W 200 Pole to a Red oak at H thence N along the Lyons Creek 220 Pole to first Station.

John Lott
George Clark } Sworn Chain Carriers

[illegible] Surveyor

[illegible] D.S.

Laid Down By a Scale of two Hundred Pole to an Inch

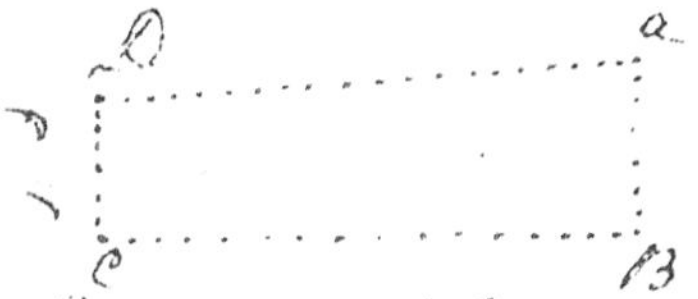

Survey'd August 1st 1778 for John Mason 10 Acres of Land according to the above Plan lying in Bute County on the waters of Shocco Beginning at McLemores Corner on Masons line a Spanish oak at the letter a thence By Masons line N 106 Pole to Danells Corner a post oak at B thence by his line & Nichols line S 10 E 32 pole to Wards Corner a white oak & pine at C thence By Wards line N 106 pole to a Spanish oak McLemores Corner at D thence By his line to first Station

Lewis Clarkam
Little B White } Sworn Chain Carriers by [illegible]

File #98

File #101

Laid Down By a Scale of two hundr[ed]
Pole to an Inch ——

Surveyed Sept 23rd 1778 for Jonath[an]
Merritt 302 acres of Land according to the above Plan lying
in Bute County on the waters of Martins Creek & [illegible] Creek
Beginning at a White oak in Garretts line at the letter A thence
N 66 pole to Rogers Corner a post oak at B thence By his line
S 83 pole to him at C thence W 117 pole to a hickory at D thence
S 223 pole to a Red oak at E on Merritts Mowbrays line thence By
the line S [illegible] 72 pole to a Black Jack at F thence E 115 pole
to a Red oak at G thence N 90 pole to a Black Jack Garretts
Corner at H thence [illegible] Garretts Corner [illegible] the same Course to
the first Station

Jn Merritt
&
Moses Falkner } Ch. Carr.

Jos Hawkins Sur.
by Wm Christmas D.S.

File #100

Laid Down By a Scale of two Hundred
Pole to an Inch ————

Surveyed Sept 30th 1778 for John Pinnell [illegible] acres
of Land according to the above Plan lying in the
County of Bute on the waters of Little Shoco
Beginning at a Black Jack In wards line at the
Letter A thence By S line W 32 Pole along
a Branch of Little Shoco & [illegible] Road to Argony
Corner In wards line at B thence [illegible] by
Argone line 44 Pole to Pinnells Corner a Black Jack
at C thence By his line E 232 Pole along
the sd Branch to a hickory then Continued 4 pole
to a Stake at D thence N to first Station

Robert Argo
&
John Irby } Chain Carr. by W Christmas D.S.

Plotted by a Scale of two
Hundred poles to an Inch

Surveyed Decemb.r 3.d 1778

For Thomas Young 640 Acres of Land
agreable to the annexed plat lying
in Burke County on the N.o Side of
Little fishing Creek beginning at a
White Oak Mosleys Corner Just on
the N.o Side of the s.d Creek at the
~~Little~~ Letter a thence by Mosley's
line N.o 51 E 220 poles to Bobbits Corner
White Oak thence by his line N. 180 poles to a black
Jack thence W.o by his line 366 poles to a Red Oak
thence by Fletchers line N.o 276 poles to his Corner
White Oak thence by s.d line W.o 110 poles to a Stake
thence N.o 210 poles to a Stake in Haylewoods line thence
S.o by s.d line 98 poles to a White Oak thence by Good-
-mans line E. 180 poles to a Red Oak thence S. by s.d line
116 poles to a white Oak thence E. by Newsoms line 232
poles to a Black Oak thence S. by Youngs old line 130
poles to a sourwood on the N. Side of Creek thence
down the various Courses thereof to the beginning

Wm Young
&
Richard Harris } S.C.C. by Wm Christmas S.

Laid Down By a scale of two hundred Pole to an Inch

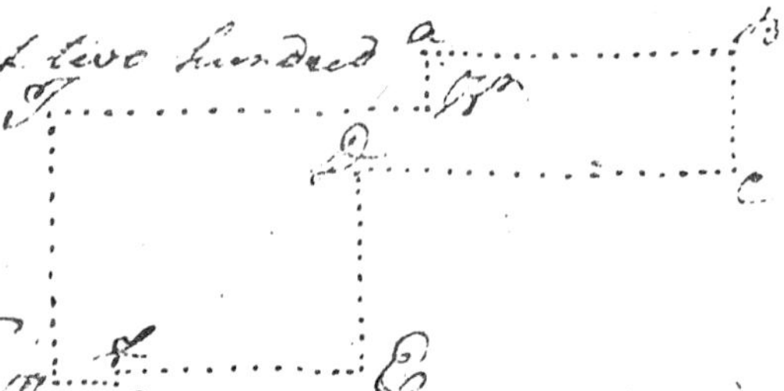

Surv.d Octob.r 21st 1778 for Benj.n Ellefs 450 acres of land according to the above plat lying in Bute County on Waters of Sandy ... Beginning at Youngs Corner In Glovers line at a stake at the stake A thence E. By Youngs line E. 40 pole to a pine in tithts line at B thence By his line S. 95 pole to a Stake On Ellefs line at C thence By his & towns line W. 294 pole to a white oak towns Corner at D thence By towns line S. 152 pole to Ellefs Corner a Spanish oak at E thence By his do line W. 198 pole to a pine on the N. Side the old Trading Road at F thence S. 11 pole to Johnsons Corner a white oak at G thence By Johnsons line 14 pole to a hickry at H thence N. 250 pole to a Red oak at I thence W. 30 pole along ... Branch to Glovers Corner a white oak & thence By his line the same Course ... pole to a hickry at K thence to the first station

Abraham Childress
&
Jn.o Glover Ch. Car.s

Jo.s Hawkins ...

BUTE COUNTY LAND ENTRIES

1. Warrant issued 16 June 78

Bute Co.
Wm Denson enters 640 A on waters of Peachtree & Cyrpess adj. Bell's line, Webb's line, Wilson's line, Park's line, Simmon's line, Carr's line then cross the vacant land to Bell's line.
16th March 1778 Wm Denson

2. W issued 16 June 78

Bute Co.
William Denson enters 260 A adj. Bell's line, binding on my other entry, including the Forks of Iveys and Farrells Road & thence to Carr's.
16th March 1778 Wm Denson

3. W issued 16 June 78

Bute Co. William Denson enters land on the Branches of the little Cypress, joining Henry Hunts line & Wm Wards line for the complement of 300 A.
16th March 1778 Wm Denson

4. W issues 16 June 1778

Bute Co.
Jesse Mabry enters 940 A on the north side of Tarr River upon th said River & the waters of Bear Swamp, little swallow & the pig pen Branch, adj. my own line, Mabry's line, Person's line, B---- line, Ivey's line & Rosses line.
16th March 1778 Jessee Mabry

5. W issued 16 June 78

Bute Co.
Henry Pope enters 640 A on the south side of Tarr River on waters of the Buffello & little Creek adj. Mabry's line, Benjn Sewells line, & Park's line.
16th March Henry Pope

6. W issued 16 June 78

Bute Co
Thos Nelmses entry adj. Wm Park's line on the Branches of the Cypress thence to Wilson's line on the Branches of Peachtree for the complement of 640 A.
16th March 1778 Thos Nelms

7. Thos Cook Caveat Wart. iss. as P Order Court 25 Sepr 1779 Issd. a second wart. 4 March 1782 the other being lost

Bute Co.
Benja. Ward enters 200 A on the Waters of Flat Branch on the south, begining at my own line & along the same to Fussell's line thence to Bagley's line, thence to my own line.
B Ward
16 March 1778

8. Jas. Denton Caveat 8 May 1778

Bute Co.
Benj. Ward enters 600 A on the west side of Weaver's Creek on my own corner adj. Hackney's line.
B. Ward
16th March 1778

9. Osborn Jeffreys Caveat Cavt. Dismissed Smith hath conveyed this entry to Jno Robinson. Wart is issued in Robinson's name 24 June 1779	Bute Co. George Smith enters 640 A on south side of Tarr River on the waters of Buffello & little Creek, adj. Jeffery's line, Park's line, & Mabry's line. Geo Smith 16 March 1779
10. W issued 16 June 78	Bute Co. Henry Pope Entry adj. wm Denson's Entry on the Branches of the Cypress & to John Simmons line a north course for the complement of 300 A 16th March 1778 Henry Pope
11. W issued 16 June 78	Bute Co. Lodiwick Alford enters 200 A begining on Ross's line, thence to Arnold's line thence to Wright's line, south side of Tarr River & on the waters of Crooked Creek including Wm Alford's Improvements. 16th March 1778 Lodiwick Alford
12. W issued 16 June 78	Bute Co. Lodiwick enters 200 A on south side of Tarr River, begining at my own line, upon the Beaver Dam. Lodiwick Alford 16th March 1778
13. George Richards Caveats the Entry of G. Hill 1 Apr 1778 W issued as P order Court 6 Apl 79	State of North Carolina Green Hill enter'd a claim for 53 A of unappropriated land in Bute Co. on the Branches of Fox Swamp, adj. sd. Hill, Wm Conyers, Bennett Hill & George Richards. G Hill 16 March 1778
14. W issued 16 June 78	Bute Co. Jas Barrow enters 640 A lying on the waters of Peachtree & waters of the little Creek begining on the south side of Thos Nelms Entry. Jas Barrow 16th March 1778
15. W issued 16 June 78 (Benjamin Westor) (Caveat 7 Aug 78) withdrawn	Edmond Denson's Entry in Bute Co. adj. William Denson's Entry & Jno Carr's line & running toward Red bud & Cabe(?) prong for 640 A Edmond Denson 16th March 1778
16. Wm Morriss Caveat 15 June 1778 W issued 21 Dec 1778	Bute Co. Michael Colins enters 640 A on waters of Sandy Creek & Red Bud adj. Davis's, Dear's Branch, Hill's line, Well's line and my own line, including one Improvement on sd. land. 16th March 1778 Michl. Collins

17. W issued 16 June 78	Bute Co. For William Green 200 A in the fork of Ivey's Road & Halifax Road, adj. GOSWICK's, Murray's & Hill's lines. 16th March 1778
18. W issued 16 June 78	Bute Co. For William Green 640 A on north side of Wm Denson's Entry on waters of Red Bud, adj. Joshua Yarbrough, Eley & others. 16th March 1778
19. W issued 16 June 78 sent by Os Jeffery	Simon Jefferys Enters 450 A in Bute Co, northerly of Buffello Run, adj. Osborn Jeffery's, Wm Mays, his own bought of White, Blakes, Saml Fullers & Henry Coopers lines including Wm Kimbrough & Wm Moseleys Improvement. 16th March 1778 Simon Jefferys
20. W issued 16 June 1778	State of North Carolina Bute Co. Henry Hill enters a Claim to 640 A on the Branch of Mill Stone Cyrpess & Cycamore adj. lines of Jos Goswick, Morgan Murray, Wm Brown, Wm Brinkley & sd Hill. 16th March H Hill
21. John Christmas Caveat W Issued as P Order of Court 24 Dec 1778 Deed sent by Jno Baxter 14 Decr 1779	Young McLemore Enters 640 A in Bute Co adj. lines Phil. Hawkins, Wm. Brock, Geo Nicholas, Jas Mills, & Jas House, on the waters of Sandy Creek Including one Improvement made by Martin Dickerson. Young Mclemore 16th March 1778
22. W issued 17 June 78	Bute Co. Young Mclemore enters 100 A adj. lines of Mathew Organ, Rd Ward, & Pennel's line on the waters of little Shoco. Young Mclemore Bute County 16th March 1778
23. W issued 17 June 1778	Young Mclemore enters 250 A on waters of Shoco & Weavers Creek, adj. lines of Seth Williams, Jas House, Ben Ward & sd. Mclemore. Young Mclemore 16 March 1778
24. Jno Griggs Caveat 9 May 78 W issued 15 Feb 79 agreable to Order Court	Saml Jones by Virtue of Improvement enters 400 A on waters of Sandy Creek, lying partly on the Buzzard Branch, adj. his own, Goswick line & Mosley's line. 16th March 1778 Saml Jones

25. W issued 17 Jun 78	Osborn Jefferys enters 640 A adj. his own line, Rays Creek, Basses & David Jefferys line toward David's Creek. 16 March 1778 Osburn Jefferys
26. W issued 17 June 1778	Osborn Jefferys enters 640 A on both sides of Crooked Creek, adj. his own lines, including Roger Reeses Improvement and toward little River. Osb Jefferys 16th March 1778
27. Wm Durham Caveat 9 May 1778 W issued as P Order of Court & sent by Son 20th Novr 1778	I Jas Nicholson do enter 640 A on waters of Stone house Creek & Hubb Quarter Creek on both sides Eaton road & Halifax Road Begn Edwd Hollimonds line, Kellies line, Wm Durhams line, Jos Shearings line, Danl Sledge's line, Newit Harriss's line , including one Improvement made by said Nicholas 16th March 1778 Jas Nicholson
28. W issued 17 June 78	Osborn Jeffery's enters 100 A south westerly of Cedar Creek adj. on all sides by his own lines. Osber Jefferys 16th March 1778
29. John Park Caveat 7th May 1778 W issd 2d June 1784	Osbern Jefferys enters 200 A on both sides Buffello Run on the southwest side Tar River, adj. Frs Mabry's, John Parks, & Benj Sewell's lands. Osb Jefferys 16 March 1778
30. W issued 17 June 78	Osbern Jefferys enters all the surplus land within his old lines on both sides of Davis's Creek an old Survey & Deed granted to sd. Jefferys by Earl Granville 300 A Os Jefferys 16th March 1778
31. W issued 17 Jun 78	Osbern Jefferys enters 500 A on both sides of Taylors Branch, southerly of Cedar Creek, joining his own lines & Dd. Jefferys. Os Jefferys 16th March 1778
32. Michael Dent Caveat 15 June at Night 7 W issued as P order Court 29 June 80	Osbern Jefferys enters 640 A near the Head of Mill Stone & Smiths Creek, adj. his own lines little River, Thos Jackson's lines including his own & Lilington Banks Improvements Osber Jefferys 16 March 1778

33. W Issued 17 June 1778	John Sàmons Jur. Entry adj. William Denson Entry on the Branches of the Cypress 300 A Jno Simons (+) 16th March 1778
34. W Issued 17 June 1778	I John Macon do enter 250 A on waters of Shoco on both sides of the Granville old Court House Road, adj. sd. Macon's line, Young Maclemore's line, Urbane Nicholson's line, Alexr Donald's line including the Crop Road as leads from Mrs. Peebles to Col. Hawkins. 16 March 1778 Jno Macon
35. Thos Garriott Caveat 7th May 1778 W Isd. 3 Apl 1780 agreable to Order of Court	John Hawkins Jr enters 640 A on Sandy Creek known by the name of Buckoms Branch & Thornton's Mill Creek, adj. lines of Edward Jones, formerly Lindsays, & Dukes, Robocks, including the improvement of Mary Weaver, the Widow Garriott, and the Widow Pendergrass, granted formerly in Lord Granville's Office for Phl Hawkins, Sal. Martân & given to the sd. Jno Hawkins by Phil. Hawkins 16 March 1778 Jno Hawkins
36. Enoch Powell Caveat 15 June 1778 at Night A second Wart. Isd 4tMar March the First being lost	John Hawkins Jr. enters 640 A on waters of Sandy Creek, Colet Thorntons Mill Creek, adj. lines of Burwell & Saml. Duke to include John Hawkins improvement whereon Jas Stowers now live including also the improvement whereon Enoch Powell lives. Jno Hawkins Jr. 16 March 1778
37. W Issued 17 June 1778	John Hawkins Jr enters by Virtue of an Improvement 30 A on borders of Sandy Creek adj. lines of Wm. Tabb, formerly the property of Chas Lyles & adj. the lines of the lands he purchased of Jas Stother & Isum Cogwell. 16 March 1778 Jno Hawkins Jr.
38. W Issued 17 June 1778	Bute Co. Benjamin Ward enters 150 A adj. Joshua Perry, Jno Grants, Jno Thorntons & Thos Hill lines. Benj Ward 16 March 1778
39. W Issued 17 June 1778 Partrick McBoyd Caveat 24 July 78 Caveat withdrawn 17th Augt 1778	Bayley Flemming enters 640 A on waters of Fishing Creek & Anderson Swamp, begining at Jas Basketts Corner, to Jno Bowdowns Corner, corner of the purchase patten land, to Lewis Ballards line, to Cauthhams line to Jos Darnals to Bower's line...Colyers Road...line of Jas Baleys. 16 March 1778 Bayly Flemming

40. W Issued 17 June 1778

March 16th 1778 Atkin Maclemore enters 500 A on waters of Fishing Creek, Reedy Branch, Beg. at Robt Williams, thence to Wm Browns, thence to William Dutys, the Widow Basketts, thence to Bass's.
16 March 1778 Atkin Mclemore

41. W Issued 17 June 78

Entered this 16th March 1778 by Atkin Mclemore 250 A begining at sd. Mclemore's corner to Col. Hawkins line...Jno Hawkins line...Sumners Corner.
Atkin Mclemore
16 March 1778

42. Wm Bragdin Caveat
Zachariah Dickson caveat
Jno Rackley Caveat
9 May 78

George Tassey enters 640 A begining at Wm Brogdens on little Buffello...corner on flat rock...Jas Wotons line...Geo Brodgens land, Chas. lipley(?) corner.
Geo. Tassey
16 May 1778

43. W Issued 17 June 1778

Thos Person Enters 640 A on waters of Stone house Creek, the marsh and Hobquarters Creek adj. his own several lines, the lines of Eaton & others
16 March 1778

44. W Issued 17 June 78

Thos Persons enters 640 A on Branches of Shoco Creek adj. his lines (the lands in dispute formerly between Roundtree Freeman and B Person) and adj. lines of others.
16 March 1778 Thos Person

45. W Issued 17 June 78

Wm Person enters 640 A on waters Bobits Branch adj. his own lines Jno Lancaster, Harriss & others.
Wm Person
16 March

46. Lawrence Lancaster Caveat

William Person Enters 640 A on waters Beef & Fishing Creek adj. his own lines and the lines of Joseph ______ & others.
Wm Person
16 March 1778

47. W Issued 17 June 1778

Wm Person enters 500 A on north side Tarr River including a survey formerly made by Francis Mabry Laps'd and afterwards resurveyed for Fredr Parker.
16 March 1778 Wm Person

48. W Issued 17 June 78

Wm Persons enters 550 A on Tar River adj. lands formerly cald Francis Mabry & the lines of others including a survey made same year for Fred Parker.
16 March 1778 Wm Person

49. John Thorton Caveat
7th May 1778
10 March 1787

Robert Hill enterd 640 A begining at Thos Hills Corner, adj. John Th**ntons, George Williamson & Dorseys Entry including Jonigans Improvement.
Ro Hill
16 March

50. W Issued 17 June 78
Caveat by Matthew Garriott 7 Augt 1778
Caveat withdrawn 17 Augt 1778
Deeded and sent by Jno Baxter 14 Dec 1779

Jno Hawkins by Virtue of an Entry given him by his Father Phi Hawkins enters 640 A on waters of linches Creek...corner of Jno Reeves, east side of Hawkins land no. to Phil Hawkins Junr land including a plantation purchsed from one Nelson by Phil Hawkins.
16 March 1778 Jno Hawkins

51. ___Ball caveat
600 A
Phil Hawkins caveat
At the request of Wm. Forkner, this warrant issd. in the name of Morriss(?) Jinkins 25 March 1780(?).

Wm Forkner enters 640 A on both sides of lick branch including an improvement the sd. Forkner purchased of Nathl Forkner, adj. Phil Hawkins & the land Dl. Ball lives on.
Wm Forkner

52. Lydia Massey Caveat
12 June 78
Jas Meroney Caveat
15 June 1778

Mary Massey enters for Absilla (?) Massey 640 A formerly surveyed for Hezekiah Massey where the sd. Massey lived on the south side of Tar River
16 March 1778

53. W Issued 17 June 78
sent by Wm Richards

Lucey McGuffee enters by Improvement 300 A on waters of Bennetts Creek, adj. Richards line, Bennetts line, Denmars lâne, Jones's line & Hawkins line.
16 March 1778 Lucey McGuffee

54. W Issued 17 June 78

Jno Riggan 700 A on east side of Little Creek, the waters of Hub Quarter, beg. Jas Mârrick's line, Durham's line...Jos Shearing line Mrs. Johnson's line...Thos Reed line.
Jno Riggan

55. Samuel Morriss Caveat
7 May 78
Land got by Morriss

Jno Short enters 540 A by virtue of former entry made in Earl Granville's Office by Phil Hawkins adj. lines of Roland Wilson, Powell, Rivers & Williams...on Macon(?) & Turkey Branch including impeovements made by Chas Black now in possession of Samuel Morriss & the Huckleberry Pond.
16 March 1778 Jno Short

56. W Issued 17 June 78

Jno Short enters 500 A on waters Rockey Creek & Anderson Swamp, adj. lines of William Walker, Jas Cauthan, Jno Cauthan, & Jos Darnal, Lewis Ballards line including sd. Short's improvement
Jno Short

57.	W Issued 17 June 78	Partrick McBoyd by Virtue of Improvements enters 250 A on Fishg. Creek adj. the purchase patten line, his own line; thence along Stoney Ridge path to the old Court House Road...Wrigings Ridge path ...Ballards line. Patrick McBoyd 16 March 1778
58.	W Issued 17 June 1778 Wm Tabb Caveat 14 Aug Caveat admiadmitted by the court got 600 A	Subscriber claims a right to enter 640 A with improvements...Shugar Jones old line, Col. Hawkins line, Wm. Clemmin's line, Col Sumner's line, Jno Macon's line. 16 March 1778 Benj Cimball
59.	W Issued 17 June 78	George Allen Enters by Virtue of Improvement 640 A on Sauls Creek, adj. his own line, Mrs. Johnston's line, Barnhams line, & Robt Collers line & Jno Dukes line. 16 March 1778 George Allen
60.	W Issued 17 June 78	Arthur Smith enters 100 A adj. lines of the late B Person decd, bounded by Stone House Creek, Col. Thos Eatons line including Stone Creek Marsh. Arthur Smith 16th March 1778
61.	Jas Bayley Caveat 8 May 1778 W Issued as P Order of Comrt 24 Novr 1778	Phil Hawkins Jr Enters 640 A by Virtue of improvement purchased of Jas Kimbell lying on waters of Fishing Creek, adj. lines of Wm Earls, Widow Baskett, William Duty, Jas Baskett, thence to Granville's line. 16 March 1778 Phil Hawkins Jr.
62.	Wt. Issued 18 June 78	Bute Co. 16 March 1778 Phil Hawkins Jr enters 640 A adj. sd. Hawkins line and bounded by lines as formerly survey'd on the waters of linches Creek including an improvement. Phil Hawkins Jr.
63.	Thos Pain(?) Caveat 6th May 1778 Thomas Garriott Caveat 7th May Jas Duglass Cavt 7th May 78	Charles Asque enters 400 A on waters of Flat Rock adj. Jno Arnolds new Entry & Zachariah Dicsons entry & Hawkins lines. 16th March 1778 Chas. Asque
64.	W Issued 18 June 78	John May enters 300 A on waters of Six pounds & Hawtree adj. lines of Paine, JONES & others. Jno May 16 March 1778
65.	Wt. Issued 18 June 1778 Sent by Wm Guinn __ Augt 1778	Charles Askew enters 640 A on waters of Linches Creek adj. Phil Hawkins line, Jones's corner, to include an improvement sd. Jno Hawkins purchased of Daniel Cauthorn(?). 16th March 1778 Charles Askew

66. Wt. Issued 23 Jan 1783
Esrom Cogwell
Caveat
John Arnold Caveat
13 June 1778
Rd. Jones Cavt 10 Feby 79

Aaron Fussell Enters 640 A on waters of Dandy Creek begining at Bagley's corner, --- line, Hawkins line, including two improvements.
March 16, 1778 Aaron Fussell

67. Phil Hawkins Caveat
15 June 1778
W issued as P Order
Court 24 Novr 78

Enter in Bute Co on waters of Sandy Creek, on the north side... Gooding's line, Elias Dorsey's line...Jno Ferrells line...100 A
16 March 1778 Solomon Dorsey

68. Jas Baley Caveat
8 May 78
W Issued as P order
of Court 24 Novr 1778

James Baskett enters 300 A adj. Basketts line... waters of Fishing Creek, includimg the tiny branch
March 16th 1778 James Baskett

69. W Issued 18 June 78

James Baskett Enters 640 A adj. Phil: Hawkins line on waters of Linches Creek & Sandy Creek including an improvement made by Michael Guartney the other by Dines(?) Weldon and a pace known as the Grassey Pond.
James Baskett

70. W Issued 18 June 78

John Edwards Enters 575 A beg. Isaac Colliers line along Jacob Crohers line to Ben Seawells to James Huckabys then to George Bairds line to Bells line to Tabb's line.
Bute Co. John Edwards
March 16 1778

71. Thos Power Caveat
11 June 1778
John Gwin Caveat
11 June 1778
Morris Ramsey (?) Caveat
11 June 1778
W Issd. 25 March 80
agreable to Ord: Ct.

By virtue of two improvements JAMES HUCKABY enters 640 A Beg. in an old line called Morris Rackey's...to Joseph Williams's line to Colliers to Tabb's thence to Raileys line.
March 16. 1778 James Huckaby

72. Jno Richards Caveat
15 June 1778
W Issd 22 April 85

Drury Perry Enters 640 A adj. Nathaniel Perrys line & Tho Perry's line on both sides Flat Rock Creek, the Eal root branch, the fort branch and one improvement made by sd. Drury Perry.
Drury Perry

73. Benj. Cook Caveat
15 June 1778
W Issued 12 Novr 78
agreable to Order of
Court

Edward Richardson Enters by Improvement 200 A on waters of Red bird Creek, adj. lines of Wells and Davis & Collins new Entry.
16 March 1778 Edward Richardson

74. Jonathan Salmon
Caveat
Given to Salmon

Samuel Bell Enters 200 A beg. at Mrs. Pattyshalls Corner thence to Hardway Davis's line to Henry Dickins line to Benj Jones' line
Saml Bell

75. W Issd. 22 May 79

John Christmas Enters 500 A on each side of the pounder branch adj. George Nichols line to Nutbush path to ------ to William Brocks & including his own improvement.
March 16 1778 John Christmas
Disputed between Christmas & Mclemore

76. John Baxter Caveat
9 May 1778
Jno Hawkins Caveat
W Issd for the remainder
22 May 79

James Burke Enters 640 A on waters of Smiths Creek, adj. lines of Robert Coller, Thomas Sales, Jonathan Johnson, Matthew Robinson
March 16 1778 James Burke

77. James Meroney Caveat
11 June 1778
Issd. 14 July 1785
in the name of
Jno Debord(?)

William Ball enters 500 A on waters of Evans's Mill Creek and Linches Creek adj. lines of Thomas Person(?), Olivers, Saml Fullers & John Stone on both sides of Simms Road & Bells Road...James Smith's line, William Smith's line, Aaron Overton's line and Roger Jones' line... made by virtue of Improvement made by Robert Ham & Jno Lewis
William Ball

78. Disputed
W Issd. Agreeable to
Order of Court 28
Augt 1780

Michael Dent Enters 640 A on waters of Richland Creek, Smiths Creek & Little River, adj. John Clayton, Thomas Jackson, Joseph McGehe & Osborn Jeffreys, including his own Improvement.
Disputed Dent & Jeffreys Michael Dent
16 March 1778

79. W Issued 18 June 78

John Mathis Enters 640 A on waters of Brandy Creek, Rays Creek, Crooked Creek, & little River adj. John Clayton & Thomas Person and Osborn Jeffreys, including his own Improvement.
John Mathis
16 March 1778

80. W Issued 18 June 67

I William Darnall do Enter 640 A on waters of Shocco and Weavers Creek...Edwd Bass's line... Rheuben Bennett's line...Col. Sumners to Young Mclemore's...Seth Williams's, including place called poke patch.

81. W Issued 18 June 78

William Truelove Enters 432 A southeast of Cedar Creek adj. Osborn Jeffrys, Josiah Reddick, & Willis Perrys lines, including his own improvement.
William Truelove
16 March 1778

82. W Issued 18 June 78

Ephraim Perry Enters 640 A on bookers Branch adj. lines of Thomas Arnold & Nathl Perry, including an improvement wheron sd. Perry lives.
Ephraim Perry
16 March 1778

83\. W Issued 18 June 78

Jesse Rowland Enters 640 A on waters of Davis's Creek adj. Osborn Jeffrys's line & Joseph Bridge's line including sd. Rowland's improvement.
Jesse Rowland
16 Mar 177-

84\. W Issued 18 June 78

Ralph Rachel Enters 640 A adj. Osborn Jeffery's, David Jeffreys, William Perrys, and Jesse Rowlands lines including his own & Mary Dent's improvements.
Ralph Rachel
16 Mar 177-

85\. Daniel Pegram Caveat 9 May 1778 Issued as P Order of Court for 517 A sent by Mr Nicholson 20 Novr 1778

Frazier Riggs enters 750 A beg. Thomas Bells corner on little Creek...Gideon Pegram's line, George Pegram's, Edward Pegram's line, Robert Harris' line, Jordan Harris' line, John Faulsons(?) line, Edward Holliman's, William Kelleys (land he bought of M. Thornton).

86\. W Issued 24 June 78

Silvanus Merrett Enters 300 A on head of Stone House Creek, beg. Edward Hollimons Croner, Lewis Patterson's line, Thomas Walkers line, Newel Harris's line.
Silvanus Merritt

87\. W Issued 24 June 78 Sent by Andr Rayley(?)

Richard Walker Enters by Improvement 75 A on Eaves Mill Creek & linches Creek adj. Eaves line, Tharrington, Richards line & Leading Jones.
16 March 1778 Rd. Walker

88\. W Issued 20 June 1778

Wm Richards enters for 300 A on both sides of Lyons Creek, beg. on John Richards line, Joseph Williams Jr line, including my Improvement.
March the 16 day 1778 Wm Richards

89\. W Issued 20 June 1778 sent by Wm Richards

John Richards Enters by Virtue of Improvt. 400 A on head of lyons Creek adj. his own line & Hawkins line.
16 March 1778 Jno Richards

90\. W Issued 24 June 78

Thos Brigers enters 640 A on long fork of Rays Creek beg. at Jefferys line on Crooked, including the improvement wheron the sd. Bridges now live.
16 March 1778 Thos Bridgers

91\. Thos Piner(?) Caveat 6th May 78 Satisfy'd W Issued --Sept 1778

Jno Thomas enters by virtue of Improvement 450 A on waters of lyons Creek on both sides of the old Spring branch adj. Mroney line, Geo Blockers line & the glebe line.
16 of March 1778 John Thomas

92. Disputed Lost — George Richards 70 A lying between George Richards lines, Green Hill lines, Conyers line, Bennett Hill lines.
George Richards
16th March 1778

93. W Issued 24 June 78 — Micajah Yarborough enters 100 A by improvement on branches of mill Stone adj. Stuarts line & his own line & his fathers Joshua Yarbroughs line.
16 March 1778 Micajah Yarbrough

94. W Issued 24 June 78 sent by Os Jeffreys — Wm Jefferys Enters 640 A on north side of little river beg. on Osbern Jefferys line, including his own Improvt on the Fort Branch.
March 16. 1778 Wm Jefferys

95. W Issued 24 June 78 sent by Os Jeffreys This warrant was assigned by Drury Jones to Wm Jeffreys Novr 1778 — Drury Jones enters 640 A on north side of little River beg. on Osbern Jefferys line including his own improvement on the Bever Dam Branch.
Drury Jones
16 March 1778

96. W Issued 26 June 78 — Henry Hunt enters 640 A on waters of Turkey Creek, little Creek & little Peachtree adj. Hilliards line, Murdock's(?) line, Jno Taylors line, & Nathl. Whutleys line, including my own improvement.
H Hunt
16th March 1778

97. W Issued 26 June 78 — Andrew Railey enters 640 A by Improvement on lions Creek & on waters of Giles Creek on both sides of the falling Branch adj. Morris Raileys line, his own line, Cliftons line, Jno Richards line, Williams line, Hills line.
16 March 1778 And. Railey

98. W Issued 26 June 78 — William Brock enters 400 A on Sandy Creek adj. lines of Phil Hawkins, Forkner, & Christmas's to include the plantation of sd. Brock .
16th March 1778 Wm Brock

99. William Ferrell Caveat 18 May 1778 W Issd. 8 June 79 — Jno Farrell enters 640 A on So side of Tarr River on the Camp Branch, beg. at sd. Farrills line adj. Burwell Perreys & Benjn. Person's line including a hog pen upon sd. Entry.
16 March 1778 Jno Farrell

100. Osborn Jeffreys Caveat — David Mims enters 400 A on little Creek, adj. Mabry's line, Massey's line & Jefferys line on the south side of Tar River. David Mims
16th March 1778

101. Disputed	John Rackley entered 640 A on Buffello Creek, beg. on James Wooton line. 16th March 1778 Jno Rackley
102. W Issued 24 June 78	Bute Co. Joseph Merrett enters 450 A on waters of Martin's Creek & Linches Creek adj. lines of Thos Garriott Joseph Rogers &c, including two improvements. Jos. Merrett 17th March 1778
103. Abraham Smith Caveat 11 June 1778 Agreed W Issued 13 July 1778	James Merrett enters 450 A adj. Hawkins line, Edwards line & the County line, including one improvement whereon the sd. Merritt lives... on linches Creek Jas. Merritt 17th March 1778
104. W Issues 26 June 78	Thos Cook enters 100 A on waters of Shoco on both sides the Church Road near the Church, beg. at Edd. Jones' line, Richd Ward's line. Thos Cook 17 March 1778
105. Disputed This land lost	Thos Cook enters 150 A on waters of Shoco & Sandy Creek on both sides Barfords old road beg. at Wm Bagleys line, Aaron Fussell, & Ben Wards line. March 17 1778 Thos Cook
106. Gibson Martin Caveat 27 May 1778 W Issd. as P order Court 8 Apl 1779	Jno Hogg enters 640 A on waters of great Crooked Creek beg. Cerber Sanders line & Thos Sanders line to Jos Norriss's line. 17th March 1778 Jno Hogg
107. W Issued 16 June 1778	Benj Hill enters 640 A where Samson Bobo formerly lived adj. Thos Hill Junr line, Micholas Murfey's line, John Person's. 17th March 1778 Benj Hill
108. W Issued 16 June 78	Caleb Dorsey enters 640 A on waters of Sandey Creek beg. at Walley's(?) corner, Pierce's line, Jno Howels line, Benj Hill's line, Geo Williamson line, John Myrick's line, Watlie's line. 17 March 1778 Caleb Dorsey
109. W Issued 26 June 1778	John Pinnell Enters 100 A on waters of Little Shoco adj. his own line, Matthew Organ line, & Richard Wards. Jno Penell

110. This land is sold and the Entry Altered Jas Murphey Caveat 4 Apl 1778 W Issued 26 June 1778

Henry Hill (Richard Conyard written and stricken) Enters 400 A on south side Tarr River, beg. on the long branch in Maceas(?) line to Jos Bakers to James Murphy to Henry Hill.
17 March 1778 — Richard Conyers(stricken) Henry Hill

111. W Issued 29 June 78

Thomas Nelms enters 640 A on waters of Sicamore & Cypress beg. at Brinkles line then adj. Wm Denson's Entry including the great fork.
17 March 1778 — Thos Nelms

112. Disputed W Granted 640 A on the Wt Peoples Road joing. his own. Peoples not to Interfere with Fussels(?) claim on the et. of sd. Road 28 Sepr 1779

Esrom Cogwell enters 640 A beg. on Beckum's Branch to the fork near Pendergrasses field...to Bagleys line ...to Peebles line.
17 March 1778 — Esrom Cogwell

113. Disputed W Issd 7 Octr 1783

John Arnold enters 500 A by Virtue of Improvement on south side of Sandy Creek adj. Jno Hawkins line, Bagley's line, & by Cogwell's new line, not to interfere wt. Davis's entry down to Jas Waoltons line.
17 March 1778 — Jno Arnold

114. Thos Piner Caveat 200 A 11th Apl 78 W Issd 27 July 1779 as P Order Court

Jno Gwin enters 300 A at Richmonds line...down Shoco Rode to Jno Williams to Jas Huckabys(?)
17 March 1778 — Jno Gwin

115. Henry Hill Caveat 9 May 78 This land not got by' Conyers & pd him money back 24 Feby 1779

Richd Conyers enters 150 A on south side of Tarr River, beg. Thos Persons line...John Perrey's line to Henry hill's line.
17 March 78 — Rd Conyers

116. Issued 29 June 1778

Edward Scarbrough enters 500 A on waters of Seeing Glass & Sandy Creek my own former entry & survey.
17th March 1778 — Edward Scarbrough

117. W Issued 29 June 78

Jenkins Devaney Enters by Improvement 180 A on waters of Buffellow adj. his own line, Jno Tabb's line, Huccabes line & Hawkins line.
17 March 1778 — Jenkins Devaney

118. W Issued 29 June 1778

Thomas Glover enters 250 A on north side of Tarr River on waters of little Turkey Creek, adj. Henry Taylors lines & Jno Hubbards lines.
17 March 1778 — Thos (+) Glover

119. Disputed W Issued 12 Dec 78

Henry Hill Enters 400 A on South side Tarr River adj. my own line, Person's line, Jno Perry's line.
17 March 1778 — Heny hill
at 5 L

120. Disputed

Laurance Lancaster enters for 640 A beg. on Mathew Hariss's line to Chas Harriss's line & Jos Harriss's line & Jno Lancaster & Wm Person's.
Laurance Lancaster
17th March 1778

121. W Issued 29 June 78

Henry Hunt Enters 300 A on waters of little peach tree & Turkey Creek adj. Isaac Hilliards line, Henry Taylors line & my own first Entry.
Henry Huntt
17th March 1778

122. W Issued 29 June 78

Bryan Farrell enters 300 A beg. on my own line & Wils. Perry's line on the north side of Crooked Creek.
17th March 1778 Bryan Ferrell

123. W Issued 29 June 78

John Mosley enters 150 A beg. at my own corner to Gossett's line along the Road to Hill's line.
18th March 1778 Jno Mosley

124. W Issued 29 June 78
sent by Jno. Rackley

James Smith Senr entered 50 A beg. at Wm Smith's line, Jno Stone's line, William Smith's corner.
18 March 1778 Jas Smith

125. W Issued 29 June 78

Edward Freeman enters 640 A on no. side & waters of Crooked Creek including his own improvement bought of Branderway.
18 March 1778 Ewd Freeman

126. W Issued 29 June 78

Edward Freeman enters 200 A adj. his other Entry, waters of Crooked Creek & Sider Creek.
18th March 1778 Ed Freeman

127. W Issued 29 June 78

Thos Arendell enters 600 A on waters of Crooked Creek adj. Jno Youngs, Ephm Perry & Widow Young. including sd. Arendell's improvement.
Six head Right Thos Arendell
17th March 1778

128. W Issued 29 June 78

Joseph Wright enters 640 A on waters of Crooked & Sedar Creek adj. his own Ferrell's, Perry's & Person's lines.
19th March 1778 Jos Wright

129. W Issued 29 June 78

Wm St John enters 640 A on waters of Anderson's Swamp & Fishing Creek, beg. at Jorden's corner & down Turden line to Tabbs Corner to Basketts.
19 March 1778 Wm St John

130. Stephen Beckam Caveat 11 May 1778 W Issd. 20 Augt 1779 agreeable to Order Court A second wart. Issd. 4 March, first being lost	Merriman Thorne enters 640 A on waters of Weavers Creek & head of Fishing Creek, beg. at Seth Williams' line to the Widow Basketts...Tabb's line including an improvement made by sd Thorne. 19 March 1778 Merr. Thorne
131. W Issued 13 July 78	Thomas Thorne enters 640 A on waters of Weaver's Creek & Sandy Creek, beg. at Arthur Jordan line at the Granville County line, Wm Tabb's line (formerly Hobbs) thence Robt Williams', Dentons, Col. Phil Hawkins, Wm Brocks, including an improvement made by Jas Lawhorn &c. 19 March 1778 Thos Thorne
132. W Issued 13 July 78 Thos Sherrod is desirous that the Deed for this Entry may be in the name of John Cheaves 10 June 82 Test Wm Green	Thomas Sherrard enters for 640 A on both sides Tarr River beg. at Jno Ferrell line including improvement made by Thos Jones 19th March 1778 Thos Sherrard
133. W Issued 26 Augt 1778	Zachariah Dickson enters 640 A by virtue of one or two improvements beg. at Jos Williams, Edward Young's line, Devaneys line, to little Buffello up flat Rock Creek. 20 March 1778 Zac Dickson
134. W Issued 26 Augt 78	Zachariah Dickson enters 200 A by virtue of one improvement adj. his other entry. 20th March 1778 Zachariah Dickson
135. W Issued 13 July 1778	Mathew Garriott enters 400 A on south side Lick Branch, adj. Dukes line, Phil Hawkins line, Phil Hawkins Jur line,with his improvement. 21st March 1778 Mat Garriott
136. Disputed	Thomas Garriott enters 400 A on south side of Roger Thorntons Mill Creek including sd. Garriotts Improvement & Thos Cannon's(?) improvement. 21 March 1778 Thos Garriott
137. W Issued 19 July 1778	Rush Bledso enters 640 A on waters of lyons Creek, adj. Browning Williams's, Thos Hills, Benj. Hills, Jas Mills, Enoch Stringfellow & Jas Meroneys lines. 21st March 1778 Rush Bledso
138. Phil Hawkins Caveat 15 June 1778	Osborn Ball enters 600 A on both sides the lick Branch beg. on line of Phil. Hawkins including the improvement of Wm Forkner purchased of Nathl Forkner. this 21 March 1778 Osborn Ball

139. W Issued 13 July 78	Marcus Gilliam enters by improvement 640 A in Bute County on waters of Red Bud adj. Coock old line, Yarbroughs entry. 21 March 1778 Marcus Gilliam
140. W Issued 13 July 78	Robert Goodloe enters for 262 A on waters of Richland Creek & Smith's Creek adj. Goodloe's line & Jonathan Davis's which land is improved. 21 March 1778 Robt Goodloe
141. Saml Taylor Caveat 11 June 1778 Peter Brinkley Caveat 11 June 78 W Issued as P order Court 24 Nov 78	Thos Young enters 640 A on waters & north side little fishing Creek...Mosley's corner, Bobbit's Corner, including his improvement. 24 March 1778 Thos Young
142. W Issued 22 Sept 78	David Jefferys enters 640 A on both sides Davis Creek, adj. Osbern Jeffreys line, including George Keith's improvement. 26 March 1778 David Jeffreys
143. Disputed W Issued as P Order Court 27 Oct 78	Wm Brogden enters 200 A adj. Jenkins Devaneys & sd. Brogdens line & the south side of little Buffello Creek, including one improvement. 27 March 1778 Wm Brogden
144. Joseph Norriss Caveat 27 May 78	James Cone enters 200 A on south side Crooked Creek beg. on Jos. Norriss' line to Lambert's line. 1 April 1778 James Cone
145. W Issued 15 Sepr 78	Henry Fits enters 200 A on waters of Hawtree Creek adj. lines of Ellis, Gilreath, Devaney & improvement. Henry Fits 4th April 1778
146. W Issued 15 Sepr 1778	Benjamin Ellis enter'd 450 A on waters of Hawtree Creek adj. Youngs line, Fits, Edwd Ellis, Towns, & Jesse Ellis & Glover. Benj. Ellis 4th Apl 1778
147. W Issued 15 Sepr 1778	William Ellis enters 450 A adj. Benj Ellis's Entry, Glovers line, Persons, Nicholas Thornton, Edwards & Johnston. Wm Ellis 4th Apl 1778
148. W Issued 22 Sepr 78	James Murphrey enters 640 A lying on south side of Tarr River on waters of Woolf Pit Swamp beg. on Hill's line, Bakers line, Persons line, Birds line, my own line, Straughters line, to include two improvements. 4 Apl 1778 Jas Murphrey

149. W Issues 22 Sepr 78	John Thornton enters 640 A beg. on John Carr's line on the head of Cypress, including James Murrays Impt. 4 Apl 1778 Jno Thronton
150. Disputed W Isd. 25th July 1779 so as not to interfere with S-- Jones land contrary to Verdict of a Jury had	John Griggs enters 640 A an Impt made by Jno Mallaby in the year 1778 on waters of Wild Cat Branch adj. Woolbanks, Gossets line, Moseleys line, Joyners line, Fosters line & a line where Allen Monjoy formerly lived, Rainwaters line, Westbrooks line & John Gants line. 8 Apl 1778 Jno Griggs
151. W Issued 22 Sepr 78	John Ellington enters 640 A adj. the County line & between Hawtree & Smith's Creek, beg. at Ed Davis line, Ross's line, Hansells line, Kings line, Jones' line, Dickins's line. 8 Apl 1778 Jno Ellington
152. W Issu'd 22 Sepr 78	James Jones enters 120 A on waters of Hawtree beging. upon Henry Dicken's line, Jones' line, Ross's line including my own improvement. 8 Apl 1778 Jas Jones
153. W Issued 10 July 1778	Christopher Butler enters 640 A on waters of Peachtree beg. at Thos Babbs line, Jno Taylors line, Elias Gay's line, Farrells Road, including one improvement. 9 Apl 1778 Chrisr Butler
154. Disputed W Issues agreeable to Order of Court 15 May 1779	Thos Piner enters 200 A beg. on John Williams Corner, on the Glebe line, the Road, Richmond's line, including my own improvement. 11 Apl 1778 Thos Piner
155. Rebecca Perrey Caveat Wart Isd 10 March 1783 agreeable to an Order of Court Warren	Thos Arendell enters 200 A on waters of Crucked Creek, adj. my own line and the widow Weathers line, including my own Improvement. 20th Apl 1778 Thos Arendell 100 acres at 5 L
156. Disputed	Rebecca Perry enters 640 A on waters of Jumping Run & Rogers Branch beg. at Thos Arendells Corner ...Widow Weathers line to Nathl Perrys line, Wm Sanders line. 22d Apl 1778 Reca Perry
157. War Issued 13th Oct 78	George Sorrell enters 640 A on waters of lyons Creek beg. at Geo. Wootons Corner, to Jno Huckabys Corner, to Jno Williams, Collers line, including three improvements. 24 Apl 1778 Geo Sorrell

158. War Issued 13th Oct 78	Joseph Williams enters 640 A on waters of Lyon Creek beging. on Collers line adj. George Sorrells entry, including one Improvement. 24 Apl 1778 Jos Williams
159. Disputed Wart Issued 31 Augt 1779 agreeable to the Verdict of a Jury got 173 acres	Benj. Cook enters 640 A on No side red Bud Creek, beg. at Collers line to Well's line, to Richardsons line, Charles Cooks line, including one Improvement. 25 Apl 1778 Ben Cook
160. Disputed (stricken) W Issued 27 Sepr 78	Benjamin Wester enters 640 A beg. at a corner of Nelms & my own thence to Yarboroughs & Axr. Westers, Wm Denåons & Thos Davis's entry, including one Improvement 25 Apl 1778 Ben Wester
161. W Issued 22 Sepr 78	Jacob Cook entry for 300 A begining at a Turkey Oak, Davis's line, John Nazarah's line. 4th May 1778 Jacob Cook
162. Burrell Perrey Junr Caveat 3d July 78 Mr. Potter gets no land as P Certificate from Court Pd him his money 12 Novr 1779	Daniel Potter's entry for 300 A beg. at Jeremiah Perrys upon the head of Jumping Run... John Perry's line. 4 May 1778 Danl Potter
163. W Issued 25 Augt 78 sent by Lunsford	Jessee Roland enters 100 A on waters of Cedar Creek, adj. Jas Perry's & Persons line, including Wm Heads Improvement. 4 May 1778 Jessee Roland
164. Jas Duglass Caveat 7 May 1778 This land is conveyed' to Geo Taper and at the request of Thos Piner the warrt hath issued in the sd. Tapir's name 20 Decr 1780	Thomas Piner enters 640 A by Virtue of an Improvement known by the name of McIntoshes...Devaney's line...across the little Buffellow, Geo. Tapie's line. 6th May 1778 Thos Piner
165. W Issued 22 Sepr 78 as P order Court Disputed (stricken) Deed 155 acres	Jonathan Salmon enters 200 A on waters of Hawtree ...Henry Studivans line, Bullards line, Hardiways Davis's line, Henry Dickins & Jas Jones Entry to Ben Jones' Corner. 6th May 1778 Jnoa Salmon
166. Phil Hawkins Caveat 4 Augt 78 Wart Issd 17 Augt 79 agreeable to Order of Court	Samuel Morriss enters 540 A on Macons Branch adj. Wm Rolands line, Weldens & Powells & Wiggans & John Williams lines, including the Improvements whereon the said Morriss now lives. 7th May 1778 Saml Morriss

167. Disputed

Thomas Garriott enters 500 A on east side of Roger Thorntons Mill Creek, beg. on Brittain Dukes line, including two improvements...the above land is where Mrs. Barriott & Mrs. Pendergrass now live.
7th May 1778 — Thos Barriott

168. Disputed

Enoch Powell enters 300 A on waters of Sandy Creek & Thorntons Mill Creek, beg. at Hawkins line, then up a former agreement between sd. Powell & Pines Walden...to include Powells Improvement.
7th May 1778 — Enoch Powell

169. W Issued 24 Augt 78

George Mills enters 250 A beg. on John Richards...William Richards line to Zachariah Dicons line.
7th May 1778 — Geo Mills

170. Disputed

John Thornton enters 640 A beg. at Thos Hills Corner & adj. sd. Thornton, Geo. Williamson's & Dorseys Entry including Jornigans Improvement.
7 May 1778 — Jno Thornton
9 Head right

171. Disputed
W Issd. agreeable to Order Court 19 Jany 1786

James Duglass enters by Virtue of one Improvement 300 A on the fork on Great Buffallow, adj. John Ralleys Entry.
7th May 1778 — Jas Duglass

172. Disputed
W Issd. 20 March 1788 by P Goodwin --?

John Park enters 200 A on both sides of Buffellow Creek on the south side of Tarr River, adj. my own line & Seawell & Mabry to include the improvement bought of William Head &c.
7th May 1778 — Jno Park

173. W Issued 22 Sepr 78

Wm Andrews enter 400 A on waters of Tarr River & the Cypress in Jno Butlers line...Simon Williams line, Jacob Powell & the River to Butlers, including one improvement.
7 May 1778 — Wm Andrews

174. Disputed
W Isd. 22 May 79

James Bayley enters 640 A on waters of Andersons Swamp & Fishing Creek lying at John Boway(?) corner, to Basketts line across the Piney Branch & binding on the county line, one improvement.
8th May 1778 — Jas Baley

175. W Issued 22 Sepr 78

Moses Harriss enters 150 A on waters of Great Fishing Creek...Thos Hill's corner...Davis's line...Green's line, including my own improvement.
May 8 1778 — Moses Harriss

176. W Issued 11 Sepr 78	Jas Solomon enters 360(?) A on waters of Great Peachtree adj. Thos Babbs line, Geo P---- line, Henry Taylors line, includ my own Improvement May 8th 1778 Jas Solomon
177. Disputed W Issued pursut. to Order Court 16 Novr 1778 by D. Hall	James Denton enters 640 A on little Creek beg. on my own corner, to Joseph Hackneys, James House, Benjamin Wards, include my own improvement. 8 May 1778 Jas Denton
178. Disputed	Stephen Beckam enters 250 A on waters of Weavers Creek on a Branch call'd Jesseys Branch...Seth Williams Corner...Edwd Bass's corner...to the Road/..Dentons line...Joseph Hackney's.... 8 May 1778 Stephen Beckam
179. W Issued 22 Sepr 1778 Disputed W Issued as P Order Court 24 Novr 78	John Baxter enters 500 A on waters of Malone Mill adj. lines of Benj. Dukes, Jonathan Johnston & Robt Callior, include the Improvement I bought of Jno Ren(?). 9 May 1778 Jno Baxter
180. Osbern Jeffreys Caveat W Issd. as P Order 8 Apl 1779	Jessee Mabry enters 300 A on waters of Buffellow & little Creek adj. lines of Jefferys & Park & Smith's entry on both sides of the New Road. 9th May 1778 Jessee Mabry
181. Disputed W Issd. 6 June 1779 as P Order Court	Daniel Pegram enters 223 A on waters of little Hub Quarter Creek being one half of a survey formerly taken up by Joseph Riggan & Daniel Pegram including one Improvement. 9th May 1778 Daniel Pegram
182. Disputed	William Durham Enters 320 A on waters of little Hub Quarter and Stone House Creek on both sides of Eatons & Halifax Roads adj. lines of Hollaman Kelleys, said Durhams, and others, one improvement. 9 May 1778 Wm Durham
183. W Issued 22 Sepr 78	Jordan Rowland enters 640 A on waters of falling Creek beg. at Waldens line, to Rolands line, Doolings, Goalds & Hudsons, one improvement. 11 May 1778 Jordan Rowland
184. Thos Person caveat	Giles Bowers 100 A on waters of Tarr River, adj. lines of Thomas Smith, my own, & Jessee Bowers. 11 May 1778 Giles Bowers
185. W Issued 22 Sepr 1778	Moses Carr enters 50 A on waters of Kings Creek beg. Thos Woodleys Corner, Benjamin Smiths Corner, Capt Stone's line. 11 May 1778 Moses Carr

186. W Issued 22 Sepr 78
526
got 417 acres
109

James Morriss enters 526 A on waters of Richland Creek, Joes Creek & Sider(?) Creek adj. Robt Goodloe, William Liles, Thos Bell, Isaac Winstead his own line, James ----, Thos Person and County line, & improvement which Robert Goodloe bought of Bullock & Lanier & sold to sd. Morriss.
11 May 1778 Jas Morriss

187. W Issued 25 Augt 78

Linum Lunsford enters 300 A on waters of Crucked Creek, beg. at James Youngs line, Thomas Arnolds including my Improvt.
11th May 1778 Linum Lunsford

188. W Issued 1 Sepr 1778
Delivered himself

Charles Darnall enters 640 A on soutn side of Cedar Creek on porches branch, Joseph Rights Corner, imcluding 2 Improvements.
11th May 1778 Charles Darnall

189. W Issued 22 Sepr 78

Harbert Hanes enters 200 A on waters of Roanoak River adj. hi s own & lines of Burrell Robenson, Whites & others, including his Improvement.
12 May 1778 Har: Haynes

190. W Issued 15 Sepr 1778

James Hills enters 100 A between lines of James Egerton, Wilmont Egerton, Jno Egerton & Jas Harriss.
12 May 1778 Jas Hills

191.W Issued 22 Sepr 78
As P Order Court

Jno Hawkins enters 640 A on both sides of Hichoe Road beg. at Collers, Dukes, Jonathan Johnstons , Martin Dye
12th May 1778 Jno Hawkins

192. W Issued 22 Sepr 78

William Hansell enters 550 A on waters of Smith's Creek and Melones Mill Creek, beg. Ward's corner, Nicholson, Robinson line.
12 May 1778 Wm Hansell

193. W Issued 30 Augt 78 &
sent by Chas Asque

James Ransome enters 150 A beg. at Macons corner, Hawkins corner.
12th May 1778 Jas Ransom

194. Disputed

Thos Person enters 100 A on no side Tar river adj. lines of Giles Bowers, Jessee Bowers, & others including part of a former Entry made in Lord Granvills Office
13 May 1778 Thos Person

195. W Issued 22 Sepr 1778

William Guttery enters 200 A on both sides of Woolf Branch, adj. Wm Sprunts line & county line.
13 May 1778 Wm Guttery

196. W Issued 22 Sepr 78

Benjamin Brewer enters 200 A on waters of Cypress adj. my own line & Farrells.
15th May 1778 Benj. Brewer

197. Disputed W Issued 8 June 79	William Ferrell enters 640 A on So side Tarr River, adj. Jno Ferrell, Jno Cheaves, Julas Alford, Benj. Person & Burrell Perrey's lines, including his Improvement. 18 May 1778 Wm Ferrell
198. W Issued 22 Sepr 78	Job Self enters 100 A on waters of Mill Creek adj. his own, Wm Perrey's & Bodines lines, including an Improvement Bought of West. 20th May 1778 Job Self
199. W Issued 22 Sepr 78	Jacob Bass enters 640 A on waters of Sandy Creek, beg. at Gallen's line, to Mat Thomas's, to Davis's line. 20 May 1778 Jacob Bass
200. W Issued 15 Sepr 78	Jno Lancaster enters 640 A on waters of Bobbits Branch &Buf Creek beg. at Nathl Harriss Corner to Mathew Harriss's line including 3 Improvts. 20 May 1778 Jno Lancaster
201. W Issued 22 Sper 1778 Mr. Joshua Yarbrough hath sold this Entry to Eli Eley & requested the return of his wart to issue in Eli Eley's name 3d Apl 1780	Joshua Yarbrough enters 640 A on waters of Red Bud adj. his own, Wm Hills line & including three Improvements as P former Survey. 25 May 1778 Joshua Yarbrough
202. Mistake Entd. twice	Harbert Haynes enters 200 A on waters of Roan Oke adj. Thos Carrell, Wall, Burrell Robinson, John White & the land he purchased of Lewis 26th May 1778 H. Haynes
203. Disputed W Issued agreeable to Order Court 2d Feby 1779	Joseph Norriss enters 250 A on south side of little Crooked Creek beg. at Jno Martins corner... county line, Joseph Whealers line, including his imprt. 27 May 1778 Jos Norriss
204. Disputed Lost	Gibson Martin enters 300 A on No side of little Crucked Creek, John Martin's line, Jos Norriss's line, Kirby Sanders's line, including his Improvement. 27 May 1778 Gibson Martin
205. W Issued 19 Sepr 1778	Thos Vinson enters 400 A on waters of Crooked Creek adj. Jeffreys line & Bridgersline & including his Imprt. 5 June 1778 Thos Vinson
206. W Issued 22 Sepr 78	Joseph Mangum enters 90 A on waters of Thos Martins Creek, beg. at Christmass's corner, Ball's line, Forkners line, County line, including one Improvement. 6th June 1778 Jos Mangum

207. W Issued 24 Nov 1778	William Mathis enters 400 A on waters of Hawtree & Falling Creek, adj. Davis's line, Edward's line, Brinkleys line & Jas Dooling line including one Impt. 8th June 1778 Wm Mathis
208. W Issued 14 Oct 78	French Haggard enters 375 A on waters Buffello & Linches Creek adj. lines of Jos Leeman, Jno Merritt, Saml Fuller, Roger Jones, Jno Finch, Thos Smith & the County line including his Improvement. 8 June1778 French Haggard
209. W Issd. 8 June 79	Solomon Batchelor enters 475 A on waters of little Peach tree adj. Isaac Hilliard's line, including his improvement. 8 June 1778 Solomon Batchelor
210. Jno Driver Caveat 25 Augt 1778 Wat Issd. 22 Jany 1782 in the name of Jas Bradley by consent of Jos Batchelor Teste W Green	James Bradley(written over Joseph Batchelor, wtricken) enters 250 A on waters of Turkey Creek adj. lines of Henry Taylor & William Andrews including his own improvement 8 June 1778 Jas Bradly Joseph Batchelor (stricken)
211. W Issued 15 Sepr 78	Abraham Smith enters 200 A on waters of linches Creek, adj. lines of Denl Edwards, Joseph Rogers, & the county line including 2 improvements. 11th June 1778 Abraham Smith
212. W Issued 15th Sepr 78	Roger Thornton enters 200 A on waters of Weaver's Creek, adj. lines of Wm House & Benj Ward. 11th June 1778 Rober Thornton
213. Disputed Lost	Samuel Taylor enters 125 A on waters of little fishing Creek adj. lines of Alston Bobbitt & Taylors lines including one Improvement. 11 June 1778 Saml Taylor
214. Disputed Lost	Peter Brinkley enters 30 A on waters of little fishing Creek adj. Bobbits and Taylors lines including one Improvement. 11 June 1778 Peter Brinkley
215. Disputed	Morriss Railey enters 640 A on Cimbrough's & long Branches adj. lines of Joseph Williams, Colliers, Tabbs & his own & Richmonds lines, including 3 Improvements 12 June 1778 Morriss Railey

216. W Issued 28 Jany 69

Thomas Turpin enters 60 A on No side Tarr River adj. lines of his own, Claxton and Mabrey formerly surveyed by Thos Persons.
13 June 1778 Thos Turpin

217. Disputed
W Issued as P Order Court 11 Jany 79

Lydia Massey enters 640 A on So. side Tarr River as formerly Surveyed for Hezekiah Massey adj. lines of Goodloe Hudmons, Massey, including her Improvt.
13th Lydia Massey

218. Disputed
Wt Issd.
6 Arpl 1785

John Richards enters 640 A on waters of Flat Rock Creek adj. lines of Jno Perry & Nathl Perry including his Imprevts.
15 June 1778 Jno Richards

219. Disputed

Philn Hawkins enters by Virtue of a former entry made 23d Feby 1763 150 A on both sides Sandy Creek adj. lines of Jno Terrell, Wm Woodard, Goodings, Elias Dorsey &c.
15 June 1778 Phill. Hawkins

220. Disputed
Wart Issd. 25 March 1780 agreeable to Order of Ct.

Phil Hawkins by an improvement purchased of Nathl Forkner Enters 320 A adj. lines of Phil Hawkins Jr, his own lines, formerly purchased of Danl Ball, Thos Garriott &c. on waters of lick branch & Martins Creek.
15 June 1778 Phil Hawkins

221. W Issued 24 Novr 78

Richard Pennell enters 50 A on waters of Shoco adj. lines of Gatling & Nelms including one Improvement.
15 June 1778 Rd. Pennell

222. W Issued 25 Sept 78

Bridges Freeman enters 620 A on Anders Creek adj. lines of Alford, Jno Mullins, Wm Freeman, Saml Jones, Jno Cooley, Hartsfield, Wright, Wommock.
15 June 1778 Bridges Freeman

223. Joseph Lindsay Caveat 25 Augt 78
Lindsey is dead__
Wt Issd. 7 Feby 1785

Ephraim Vaughn enters 300 A on waters of little Peach tree adj. lines of Hilliard includg. his Improvement.
15 June 1778 Ephraim Vaughn

224. Disputed
W Issd. as P Order Court 9 Apl 79

William Morriss enters 50 A on waters of Red Bud adj. lines of Capt Collins, Frans Wells, & Montfords including one Improvement.
15th June 1778 William Morriss

225. W Issued 15 Sepr 78

Joseph Harriss enters 150 A on waters of Fishing Creek adj. lines of David & the County line on Et. side of Green's Branch.
15 June 1778 Jos Harriss

BUTE COUNTY LAND ENTRIES

No.	Warrant / Notes	Entry
226.	Disputed	James Meroney enters 400 A on waters of linches Creek adj. lines of Stone, Overton & others including this Improvement of Smith & Ham. 15 June 78 Jas Meroney
227.	Disputed by request of parties this Warrant is Issued in the Name of George Williams 14th July 1779	Jas Meroney enters 246 A on waters of Woolfpit Swamp adj. lines of Duncan, & Wm Massey including the Impt whereon Jno Davis now lives. 15 June Jas Meroney
228.	W Issued 24 Nov 78	Nathaniel Lewis enters 100 A on waters of linches Creek, adj. lines of Haggard, Highte, Crabb, Huckaby, & the county line including his Improvement. 15 June 1778 Nath Lewis
229.	W Issd 8 June 79	Cornelias Taylor enters 280 A on waters of little Turkey Creek adj. Wm Rosses line, Wm Andrews line, Jno Drivers entry, Wm Andreys formerly belonging to Goodridge Alford including his Impt. 15 June 1778 Cors Taylor
230.	Disputed Wat. Issd. 7 Feby 1785	John Driver enters for 400 A on Walter Bruce's line on waters of little Turkey Creek & Hilliards line, Henry Taylor & Wm Andrews Including his Impt. 15 June 1778 Jno Driver
231.	Disputed Wt Issd. 7 Feby 1785	Joseph Linsey enters 200 A on waters of Peach tree adj. lines of his own & Hilliards including his Impt. 15 June 1778 Joseph Linsey
232.	W Issd 8 June 79 (stricken) This land sold & inclosed in a Wart. from Wm Green to Jno Norwood No. 319 31st March 80	Theophilus Odum enters 100 A beg. at Henry Taylors line. 15 June 1778 Theo. Odum
233.	W Issued 19 Apr 1778 sent by T. Vinson No Land to be found	Adam Jones enters 250 A on heads of Davis's Creek adj. lines of D. Jeffreys Os Jeffreys & including his Improvement. 16 June 1778 Adam Jones
234.	W Issd. 8 June 79	Henry Montfort enters 550 A on both sides of Mill Run as formerly surveyed for Jno Linton 16th June 1778.
235.	W Issued 11 Jany 79	Henry Montfort enters 640 A on So side Tarr River on both sides the Chapple Road as formerly surveyed for Jno Linton. 16 June 1778

236. W Issd 8 June 79 remember the plots for the Survr.

Henry Montfort enters 640 A on No side Reedy as formerly surveyed for Jno Linton
16 June 1778 Henry Montfort

237. W Issued 26 Sepr 78

William Jeffreys enters 400 A adj. Osbern Jeffreys lines on waters of little River including the three prongs of the said River.
25th June 1778 Wm Jeffreys

238. W Issd. 8 June 79

Betsey Solomon enters 50 A on waters of Peach tree & Wild Cat Creek adj. lines of Henry Taylor, Drury Arrington & George Ren including an improvement where she now lives.
25th June 1778 Betsey Solomon

239. W Issued 12 Decr 78

Burrill Perrey enters 640 A on Branch call'd Jumping Run adj. lines of Jeremiah Perrey, John Perrey, Ben, Persons & Joseph Wright including his Improvement.
3d July 1778 Burrell Perrey Jr.

240. W Issued 6 Novr 1778

Roger Jones enters 700 A on waters of linches Creek beg. at a corner in Harbert Hights line ...Col. Hawkins line & adj. lines of Thos. Cook, Augustin Willis, his Own & Jno Hight as formerly surveyed for Geo Deboard.
7 July 1778 Roger Jones

241. W Issued 24 Decr 1778

Jethro Sumner Enters 700 A on head of Shoco and fishing Creek beg. Wards line, adj. lines of Tabb, Bëckam, the Purchase Patten, Foxes & Young Mclemore as formerly surveyed for Mathew Duty.
8th July 1778 Jethro Sumner

242. W Issued 16 Novr 78

Durham Hall enters 250 A on waters of Tarr River adj. Rāchd. Clapton(?), Seth Mabry, Chaves's & his own lines including one Impt bought of Simon Handcock.
14 July 1778 Durham Hall

243. W Issued 24 Nov 78

Robert Caller Junr enters --- A beg. at Abrm Mayfield line adj. lines of Robt Caller, Martin Dye, & Edward Simon(?) also the lands lately entered by James Burk & Jno Hawkins
20 July 78 Robt Caller Jr.

224. W Issd 8 June 79

Martin Hall enters 640 A on waters of Crooked Creek on both sides of the Road adj. lines of William Reaves, Driver, Wm Hogg and Jacob Powell Including 2 Improvements.

245. W Issd 8 June 79	Wm Stiles enters 400 A on waters of Turkey Creek adj. lines of Alford, Jeremiah Stevens, & Thomas Glover's entry including 2 Improvts. 4 Augt 78 Wm Stiles
246. W Issued 25 Novr 78	Marcus Gillam enters 100 A on waters of Red Bud & joing. lines of his Own Entry, Presley Nelms, Davis, Charles Cook & Robt Carr. 8th Augt 78 M. Gillam
247. Disputed	William Tabb enters 400 A on waters of Shoco, adj. lines of Shugar Jones, Hawkins, Clements, Sumner, Macons & Cimball according to an old warrant and survey in Earl Granville Office. 14 Augt 1778 Wm Tabb
248. Disputed (stricken) W Issd 6 June 79	Wm Durham enters 50 A adj. Isaac Acre's line, Ann Hays line, Thos Harthhorn & Jno Alston Fenning's line. 14 Augt 1778 Wm. Durham
249. Entry withdrawn no Land Money paid Garret 20 Decr 1780	Mathew Garriott enters 200 A on waters of linches Creek on the west side of Joseph Hawkins Entry adj. Jas Meritts Entry & Charles Asque Entry Mat Garriott
250. W Issued 24 Novr 78	James Miller enters 300 A on waters of Stone House Creek adj. lines of Person, and land formerly Jno Mangum now Thos Eatons. 17 Augt 78 Jas Miller
251. W Issued 9 Jany 79 two warrants issd. for this land Vizt one --- Babbs 200 A & Wm Pace 192 A land sold by Shuffield & Jas Robertson to above namd. Babb & Pace	Robert Shuffield enters 350 A on waters of Tarr River beg. at Conyers & Paces corner adj. lines of Conyers, Geo Hunt, Jas Hunt, Jacob Jones, Jas Walker, Terrell & Pace. 24 Augt 1778 Robt Shuffield
252. W Issd. 2 Decr 1779	Samuel Horton enters 200 A on waters of Prickly Pear Branch, adj. his Own, Burl. Perry, Averett & Ferrells lines. 24 Augt 1778 Sal. Horton
253. W Issd. 1 March 1785	Simon Perry enters 350 A on waters of Cypress adj. lines of Hobbs, Butler & Jeremiah Stevens including his Impt. 24 Augt 1778 Simon Perry
254. W Issued 30 Nov 1778	Jno Freeman enters 600 A on waters of Flat Rock Creek & little River adj. lines of Drury Perry, Jno Richards including his Improvt. 25 Augt 1778 Jno Freeman

255. W Issd 21 June 79

Thomas Cannon enters 200 A on both sides of Flat Rock Creek & waters of Sandy Creek adj. lines of Richards, Phil Hawkins & Zachariah Dicsons new line.
26 Augt 1778 — Thos Cannon

256. W Issued 7 Jan 79 This warrant was assigned to Wm Jeffreys by Phil Jean 2 March 1779.

Philip Jane enters 640 A southwesterly of little River adj. Osborn Jeffreys laad including his Improvement & Rockey Branch.
29 Augt 78 — P Jane

257. W Issued 7 Jany 79 This warrant was assigned to Wm Jeffreys by Phil Jane 2 March 1779

Philip Jane enters 640 A on waters of the South West side of little River adj. William Jeffreys and Osborn Jeffreys lines, including his Improvement/
29 Augt 78 — P. Jane

258. Wart. Isd. 3 Apl 80

Charles Asque enters 180 A on waters of Linches Creek beg. in Joseph Hawkins new line adj. Jas Merritt, Jos Meritt and Danl Edwards.
30 Augt 1778 — Chas Asque

259. W Issued 7 Jany 79

John Green enters 250 A on waters of Crooked Creek adj. Thomas Arendell, Osborn Jeffreys, & Linum Lunsfords lines, including his Improvement.
4 Sepr 1778 — John Green

260. Thos Frohock Caveat 11 Novr 1778 Wart Issued agreeable to Order Court 18 Novr 1782(?)

Shem Cook 600 A on south sidd of Tarr River Davis's line, Frohawks line, Milley's Creek.
4th Sept 1778 — Shem Cook

261. W Issued 11 Jany 79

Jno Tucker enters 424 A on Hill's Branch adj. Hudson Blanchitt's & Phil Alston's lines, including his Improvements.
5 Sepr 1778 — Jno Tucker

262. W Issued 11 Jany 79

George Brain enters 500 A on Hills Branch and Green's Branch adj. Davis's, Harriss's & Alston's lines including his Improvements.
5 Sepr 1778 — George Brain

263. W Issued 7 Jany 79

Moses Joiner enters 85 A on Crooked Creek adj. --- Including the Improvement he purchased of Frederick Reeves.
8th Sepr 1778 — Moses Joiner

264. W Issued 7 Jan 79

Samuel High enters 328 A on waters of Richland Creek adj. lines of JamoClayton, Wm Lyles, Jas peters, Bells, Jona Davis and his own including his Improvement.
12 Sepr 1778 — Saml High

265. W Issd. 22 May 79 — Jno Hawkins enters -- A on waters of little Creek adj. lines of Ransome, Hunt, Macon and his own.
15 Sepr 1778

266. W Issd. 22 May 79 — John Hawkins enters 100 A on the head of Fishing Creek adj. Asque, Smith and Joseph Merritts(?).
15 Sepr — Jno Hawkins

267. W Issued 7 Jany 79 — Jno Prim enters 200 A on waters of Crooked Creek adj. lines of Osborn Jeffreys.
Jno Prim

268. W Issued 28 Jany 79 — Bennett Hill enters 60 A on Bear Swamp adj. lines of Wm Conyers, Seawell and others.
21 Sepr 1778 — Bennett Hill

269. W Issd 21 June 79 — Bennett Hill enters 150 A on waters of Flat Rock & Bear Swamp adj. lines of Bledsoe, Hill and others.
21 Sepr 1778 — Bt Hill

270. Wm Mushaw Cavt as P Mushaws Entry 7 Novr 1778 Wt Issd 17th Apl 1780 by Consent — Green Hill enters 640 A on waters of Cypress & Turkey Creek Including the Imprvt. Purchased of Prissilla Easterline(?) and the Great Meadow.
24 Sepr 1778 — G Hill

271. W Issd 21 June 79 — David Vinson enters 100 A on Dear's Branch adj. his own line, Charles Cooks and others
24th Sepr 1778 — D Vinson

272. W Issued 11 Jany 79 — Jno Robinson enters 175 A on south side of Tarr River adj. Lydia Mabry Entry

26th Sepr 1778 — Jno Robinson

273. W Issued 11 Jany 79 — Jno Robinson enters 175 A on south side of Tarr River adj. Henry Montfort's Entry (on both sides of the Chapple Road).
26 Sepr 1778 — Jno Robinson

274. W Issued 30th Jany 79 This warrant was assign'd by Morgan to Osborn Jefferys 11 March 79 — Robt Morgan enters 720 A on both sides of Buffelow adj. Simon Jeffreys, Wm Mays, Thos Person, Whites, Yarbroughs, Hudson & Mowdins (?) lines.
28th Sepr 1778 — Robt Morgan

275. W Issued 30 Jany 79 This warrant was assigned by May to Osborn Jeffreys 22 March 1779. Issued a second warrant now in Jeffreys name 1 Jany 1783 the first was lost — Wm May Enters 1000 A on waters of Cedar Creek & Tarr River adj. Osborn Jeffreys, Thos Persons Alias Simon Jeffreys, Francis Mabrys and Masseys.
28 Sepr 1778 — Wm May

276. W Issd 21 June 79

Wm Green Enters 100 A on waters of Mill Stone, adj. lines of Henry Hill, Murray Boon and others.
24 Sepr 1778

277. W Issd. 21 June 79
This Land Sold to Richardson & wart. granted by consent to Him 20 Octr 79

Holowell Denson Enters 100 A on waters of Red Bud adj. lines of Francis Wells & the entries of Collens, Morriss and Richardson.
30th Sepr 1778 H Densen

278. Wm Frohock
Entry With drawn the same being deed'd Land 10th Feby 1779

John Cook enters 300 A of land on so. side of Tarr River & Both sides of Billey's Creek, adj. lines of Robt Allen, William Hutson, Jno Hutson, Wm Perrey, William Winston, and Benjamin Fuller.
3 Octr. 1778 Jno. Cook

279. Thomas Frohock
Caveat 11th Novr 1778

Shem Cook enters 300 A on south side of Tarr River, adj. lines of Wm Davis, Wm Winston, Phil. Chavis, Frohawk, & Richd Claxton(?).
3d Octr 1778 Shem Cook

280. W Issd 21 June 79

William Morriss Enters 200 A on both sides of Red Bud Creek adj. lines of Cooks new Entry Davis's, Collins, Richardsons, Wells.
12th Octr 1778 Wm Morriss

281. W Issd 21 June 79

Tommy Arendell enters 200 A on waters of Crooked Creek adj. Thomas Arendell's line and Ephraim Perrey's line.
17th Octr 1778 Tommey Arendell

282. W Issd 21 June 79

Thomas Sherrod enters 50 A on waters of Buffello on the no. side adj. lines of his own Park & Jno Nelson.
27 Octr 1778 Thos Sherrod

283. W Issd 22 May 79

Charles Hicks enters 100 A on waters of Hawtree Creek adj. lines of Jno Ellis, Jno Shearing, Jas. Pain and Jno May
30 Octr 1778 Chas Hicks.

284. Dispd.
Issd 24 July 1783

William Mewshaw enters 464 A on waters of Turkey Creek adj. Jeremiah Stevens line, Butlers line, Rosses line including two improvements.
7 Novr 1778 Wm Mewshaw

285. W Issd 21 June 79

Jno Alford enters 640 A on So. side of Tarr River on both sides of the Beaver Dam adj. lines of --- Gal Alford, Cheves, Alfords Entry, & Wm Ferrels Entry.
9 Novr 1778 Jno Alford

286. Disputed

Thomas Frohock enters 500 A on South side of Tar River Between Billey's Creek & sd. River adj. land sd. Frohock bought of Joseph Edwards & the land where Robt Parker formerly lived, now the property of sd. Frohock.
Novr 11 1778 T Fr---

287. W Issd 12 May 79

John Jones enters 540 A on No Side of Reedy Creek & Joining the Meadow Branch as formerly Surveyed for Chamberlan Hutson.
13 Novr 1778 J J

288. W Issd 22 May 79

Elisha Simms enters 640 A on waters of Smith's Creek adj. Widow Jones, Howards and Sprunts lines Including 2 Impts.
13th Novr 1778 E Simms

289. Dispd.

Richd Jones Enters 200 A on waters of Sandy Creek joing. James Bagley's line, the great Fork & John Hawkins line including his Improvement.
16 Novr 1778 Rd Jones

290. W Issd 11 June 79

Saml Fuller enters 400 A on waters of Linches Creek joining Jno Dickerson, hiw own, & Zarobabel Williamsons lines, including 2 Impts.
24 Novr Samuel Fuller

291. W Issd 21 June 79

Aaron Overton enters 550 A on waters of Kings Creek & adj. lines of Jno Stone, Benjamin Smith, & Jno Merritt including 2 Improvments.
24th Novr 1778 A Overton

292. W Issd 22 May 79

Atkins Mclemore enters 40 A on waters of Lee's Branch and adj. lines of Col Sumner, Majr Hawkins.
24 Novr 1778 Atkin McLemore

293. W Issd 22 May 79

Wm Park enters 300 A on waters of Popssum Quarter & Reedy Creek adj. his own, Duke, Green & others. including his Impt.
24 Novr 1778 Wm Park

294. W Issd 21 June 79

Michael Collens enters 50 A on waters of Red Bud adj. lines of his own, Jno Webb & Wm Kerby.
24 Novr 1778

295. W Issd 22 May 1779

Philemon Hawkins Enters 40 A on waters of Deep Creek adj. lines of Joseph Birch & his own & the County line.
25 Novr 1778 Phil Hawkins

296. W Issd 22 May 79
Deed for 247

Nathl Harriss enters 360 A on south side little fishing Creek adj. Beef Creek and old House Branch adj. Jordan Harriss line, Jno Lancasters Sterling Harriss & his Own.
3d Decr 1778 Nathl Harriss

297. W Issd 21 June 79

Jeremiah Stevens enters 640 A on waters of Cypress and adj. lines of Denbey(?), Stiles, Mewshaw, Hobbs and his own Including one Impt.
4th Decr 1778 Jer Stevens

298. Warrt. Issued 5 Apl 79
This warrant was assigned by Morgan to Osborn Jeffreys 5 Apl 1779

Benjamin Morgan Enters 800 A on both sides of Crooked Creek adj. Linum Lunsford, Joseph Bridgers, Wm Perreys, Farrells, Rachels, Vinson & Osborn Jeffreys.
7 Decr 1778 Benj Morgan

299. W Issd 22 May 79

Saml Harper enters 200 A on No side of Reedy Creek adj. lines of Jones, Persons, & Newett including his Impt.
11 Decr Saml Harper

300. W Issd. 22 May 79

Richard Acock enters 640 A on Reedy Creek on the Piney Branch adj. lines of his own, Powell, Greene, Wm Green, Tomson, &c Including one Impt & the Meeting House.
Richd Acock

301. W Issd 22 May 79

Spencer Snow enters 640 A on waters of Reedy Creek on No side adj. lines of Gill, James, Newell, Harper including 2 Impts.
11 Decr 1778 Spencer Snow

302. W Issd. 22 May 79

John Green enters 100 A adj. lines of Thos Green, Jos Perdue, Thomas Christmas & John Tanner.
16th Decr 1778 Jno Green

303. W Issd 21 June 79

Josiah Reddick Enters 600 A on waters of Cedar Creek adj. line s of Jno Lamans, Jas Perrey & Saml Williams including 2 Improvements.
16th Decr 78 J Reddick

304. W Issd 21 June 79

Jeduthan Everett enters 100 A on No Side of Tar River adj. lines of his Own, Burwell Perrey, and Saml Horton, Including his Impt.
17th Dec 78 Jeduthan Everett

305. Jno Carroll Cavt
21 Decr 78
Mr Christmas relinquishes his right of Entry Recd his money

Thomas Christmas Enters 120 A on waters of Opossum Quarter adj. lines of Edward Green, Jas. Stiles, Wm Duke and Wheeler Including the Impt where Jno Carrell now lives
19th Decr 1778 Thos Christmas

306. W Issd 21 June 79

Robert Butler enters 450 A on No side of Tarr River adj. lines of his Own, Jas Hobbs --- Alford (?), including his Improvement.
19th Decr 78 Robt Butler

307. W Issd 21 June 79

Jonas Cropling enters 300 A on both sides of Cyrpess adj. lines of Robt Butler, Jas Hobbs &c Including his Improvements.
19 Decr 1778 Jonas Cropling

308. W Issd 21 June 79

Frederick Jones Enters 640 A on waters of the Cypress adj. lines of Jno Dutily(?) Jno Gay, Nathl Wheetley &c. Including his Improvt & Jno Hubbard's
19 Decr 1778 Frederick Jones

309. W Issd 21 June 79

Elizabeth Jones enters 200 A on No side of Tarr River adj. lines of Capt Ferrell, Saml Horton, Lod. Alford & Benj. Brown Including her Impt.
19 Decr 1778 Elizabeth Jones

310. W Issd 22 May 79

Jno Carrell enters 130 A on waters of Opossum Quarter adj. lines of Wm Reddick, --- Stiles Edward Green, Geo Wheler, & Jno Davis Including his Impt.
21 Decr 1778 Jno Carrell

311. 140 @ 5 L
W Issd. 21 June 79

Isaac Hilliard Enters 640 A on both sides of Peachtree formerly Survey'd for Thomas David Including 2 Improvements.
28th Decr 1778 Isaac Hilliard

312. W Issd 21 June 79

Robt Melton enters 200 A on waters of Tarr adj. lines of the Widow Alford & including one Impt.
28 Decr 1778 Robt Melton

313. W Issd 21 June 79

John Butler Enters 200 A on waters of Tarr River adj. lines of Wm Anders's his own, Robt Melton & Robt Butlers.
28 Decr 1778 Jno Butler

314. W Issd 21 June 79
Entry and Warrant Withdrawn by Mr. Hamblet the same being deeded land

Richard Hamblet Enters 170 A on So side of little fishing Creek beg. Wm Persons line, Wm Mays line,
29 Decr 1778 Richd Hamblet

315. Withdrawn being deeded land

Thomas Person Enters 500 A for the Benefit of Thos Person the Son of Wm Person decd on Branch of Fishing & Reedy Creek adj. lines of Newel, Person, Jones & others.
29 Decr 1778 Thos Person

316. W Issued 21 June 79 — Richard Smith Enters 400 A on waters of Crooked Creek adj. lines of Wammock, Pippin &c indluding two improvements.
31st Decr 1778 — R Smith

317. W Issd. 22 May 79 — Sarah Williams Enters 350 A on Middle ground between Stone House & Hob Quarter Creek Includg the Survey purchased by Jacob Williams of Owen Myrick adj. lines of Macon, Johnston, Jones & others.
31 Decr 1778 — Sarah Williams

318. 15/ due
W Issd 21 June 79 — Shadrick Floid enters 150 A on waters of the Cypress Creek adj. lines of Wm Jackson, Willson Denson and Jno Moody, including his Improvement.
31 Decr 1778 — Shad Floid

319. This land sold to Mr. Jno Norwood & a wart. iss. in his Name for 598 A Including Odum's Entry No. 232 31st March 80 — Wm Green enters agreeable to Law 500 A on waters of great Peachtree adj. Taylor and others Including the plaintation whereon Je--- Odum lives.
31 Decr 1778

320. W Issd. 21 June 79 — Jno Alford enters 400 A on waters of little Bever Dam adj. lins of Lucey Alford Including one Impt.
31 Decr 1778 — Jno Alford

321. W Issd. 21 June 79 — Philemon Hawkins Enters(by virtue of former Entry) 188 A on waters of Sandy Creek on both sides of Bledso's branch adj. lines of Goodwin House, & Martin's old lines now Tabbs lines & Fausters line.
31 Decr 1778 — Phil Hawkins

322. W Issd 21 June 79 — Phillip Taylor Enters 200 A on waters of Crooked Creek adj. lines of Cooley, Jos Norriss, Francis Bradley, Nathl Perrey & Wm Sanders including his Impt.
31 Decr 1778 — Phil Taylor

323. W Issd 21 June 79 — Saml Jones Enters 40 A ...John Calley's Corner ...Jno Foster's line, Phil Willhite's line.
31 Decr 1778 — Saml Jones

324. W Issd 22 June 79 — Oroondates Davis Enters 640 A on Redbud Creek adj. Symmonds's, Butts's, Arrington's & McGeehees lines.
31 Decr 78 — O. Davis

325. W Issd 22 June 79 — O. Davis Enters 640 A on little Peachtree Creek adj. line of Abner Hills & others.
31 Decr 1778 — O. Davis

326. Entry withdrawn being Deeded Land

John Robinson Enters 300 A on the No side of little fishing Creek, adj. lines of Person and others including the plaintation whereon John Newell now lives.
1 Jany 1779 — Jno Robinson

327. W Issd. 22 June 79

John Robinson Enters 75 A on Reedy Creek, adj. Henry Montoforts Entry formerly surveyed for Jno Linton
1 Jany 1779 — Jno Robinson

328. W Issd 22 June 79 This Entry is sold to Jno Norwood for £ 80 specie the former wart. destroy'd & a wart issued in the sd. Jno Norwoods name this 19th Nov 1783 Test Wm Green.

Henry Pope enters 640 A on waters of Redbud Creek & the Sedar Branch adj. lines of Rose & others an old Entry formerly Surveyed for Thos Davis Decd.
1 Jany 1779 — Henry Pope

329. W Issd 22 May 79

George Haselwod Enters 300 A on No side of little fishing Creek adj. lines of his own, Wm Burrow, Jno Birch & Fennel.
2 Jany 1779 — Geo Haselwood

330. W Issd 22 May 79

Thomas Young enters 325 A on south side of Ben's Creek adj. lines of Geo Haselwood, Fitts, Hills, Michl Harris, Crafords, Fluher(?) & his own.
5th Jany 1779 — Thos Young

331. W Issd 22 June 79 No Land Money returnd

Jno Rice enters 300 A on the little Beaver Dam Swamp beg. at Alford's line.
5th Jany 1779 — Jno Rice

332. This land is sold to Pace & Babb as may more fully appear by Shuffields Entry & Pace's & Babb Warrts they including 392 A with this added 27 June 1779.

John Robinson Enters 42 A on waters of Tarr River adj. Robt Shuffields Entry
11 Jany 79 — Jno Robinson

333. W Issd 22 June 79

Jno Richards Enters 550 A on waters of Julia's Branch on the No. side of little River adj. lines of Jno Perry, the County line & Jno Richards Entry.
30 Jany 1779 — Jno Richards

334. W Issd 22 June 79

Robert Carr enters 150 A on waters of Saddy Creek adj. Entries of Jno Griggs & Saml Jones and his own line.
30 Jany 1779 — R Carr

335. W Issd 22 June 79

William Green enters agreeable to Law 100 A adj. lines of his own, Mosley, Goswick &c.
2 Feby 1779

336. W Issd 22 June 79 Entry withdrawn no Land & certificate of Surveyor's Cash pd. 8 Apl 80	Thos Bridgers enters 300 A on waters of Crooked Creek adj. lines of his Own, Jeffreys &c. 8 Feby 79 Thos Bridgers
337. W Issd 22 June 79	Roger Jones Enters 49 A adj. lines of his Own & Herbert Hights. 9 Feby 79 Rogr. Jones
338. W Issd 22 May 79	Wiatt Hawkins enters 500 A on waters of Smith's Creek adj. lines of Burfords, Saml Paskell, Emberson, Howard, Williamson & on both sides of the Road from Smiths Creek to Hammonds Ordinary. 9 Feby 1779 Wyatt Hawkins
339. W Issd 22 May 79	An Entry beg. on Christopher Robinsons line including 50 A between Houses line Isrom Cogwells & the sd. Robinsons line on the waters of Sandy Creek. 9 Feby 79 Young McLemore
340. W Issd 22 May 79	An Entry beg. on Moses Myrick's, Walker's... Harriss's, Mial Harriss, Stephen Bobbits, Edwd Ellis's, both sides of the lick branch including 150 A 9 Feby 79 Nathl Nicholson
341. W Issd 22 June 79	Jessee Mabry enters 20 A on both sides of --- adj. Mabry's line & Iveys line. 9 Feby 1779 Jessee Mabry
342. W Issd. 2 Decr 1779	Jacob Bass enters 60 A on waters of Shoco adj. line of Persons & his own. 9 Feby 79 Jacob Bass
343. W Issd 2 Decr 1779	Jessee Freeman Enters 300 A on no side little River adj. Wm Jeffreys. 10th Feby 79 Jessee Freeman
344. W Issued 10 May 79	James Coppedge Enters 200 A on waters of Peach tree adj. lines of Hall, Mitchell, Nazarah, Cook, Davis and others. 11 Feby 79 Jas Coppedge
345. W Issd 2 Decr 1779	Jno Solomon Enters 100 A on the waters of Sedar Branch adj. Jacob Cook's line, Jno Michels line, Hall's line & Ross's line & Davis's line. 15 Feby 1779 Jno Solomon

The remaining entries in the book are for Franklin County.

INDEX

(N. B. P=plat; E=entry)

Other books by the author:

Abstracts of Early Deeds, Bladen County, North Carolina, 1738-1804

Ancestors and Descendants of Charles Humphries (d. 1837) of Union District, South Carolina, 1677-1984

Anson County, North Carolina Deed Abstracts, 1749-1766, Abstracts of Wills and Estates, 1749-1795

Bute County, North Carolina Minutes of the Court of Pleas and Quarter Sessions, 1767-1779

Camden District, South Carolina Wills and Administrations, 1781-1787

CD: Early Records of Fishing Creek Presbyterian Church, Chester County, South Carolina, 1799-1859

CD: Heritage Books Archives: South Carolina, Volume 1

CD: Kershaw County, South Carolina Minutes of the County Court, 1791-1799

CD: Marriage and Death Notices from the Charleston [South Carolina] Observer, *1827-1845*

CD: Winton (Barnwell) County, South Carolina Minutes of County Court and Will Book 1, 1785-1791

Chester County, South Carolina Deed Abstracts, Volume I: 1785-1799 [1768-1799] Deed Book A-F

Chester County, South Carolina Minutes of the County Court, 1785-1799

Death and Marriage Notices from the Watchman and Observer, *1845-1855*

Deed Abstracts of Tryon, Lincoln, and Rutherford Counties, North Carolina, 1769-1786, and Tryon County Wills and Estates

Early Records of Fishing Creek Presbyterian Church, Chester County, South Carolina, 1799-1859,
With Appendices of the Visitation List of Rev. John Simpson, 1774-1776, and the Cemetery Roster, 1762-1979
Brent H. Holcomb and Elmer O. Parker

Edgefield County, South Carolina Minutes of the County Court, 1785-1795

Greenville County, South Carolina Cemeteries, Volume I

Greenville County, South Carolina Cemeteries, Volume V

Index to the 1800 Census of South Carolina

Jackson of North Pacolet: Descendants of Samuel Jackson, Sr.

Kershaw County, South Carolina Minutes of the County Court, 1791-1799

Laurens County, South Carolina Minutes of the County Court, 1786-1789

Life and Times of John G. Landrum

Lower Fairforest Baptist Church, Union County, South Carolina: Minutes 1809-1875, Membership Lists through 1906

Marlborough County, South Carolina Minutes of the County Court, 1785-1799 and Minutes of the Court of Ordinary, 1791-1821

Marriage and Death Notices from Baptist Newspapers of South Carolina, 1835-1865

Marriage and Death Notices from Baptist Newspapers of South Carolina, Volume 2: 1866-1887

Marriage and Death Notices from Columbia, South Carolina Newspapers, 1838-1860

Marriage and Death Notices from Raleigh, North Carolina Newspapers, 1796-1826
Silas Emmett Lucas, Jr. and Brent Holcomb

Marriage and Death Notices from the (Charleston) Times, *1800-1821*

Marriage and Death Notices from the (Charleston, South Carolina) Mercury, *1822-1832*

Marriage and Death Notices from the Charleston Observer, *1827-1845*

Marriage and Death Notices from the Up-Country of South Carolina as Taken from Greenville Newspapers, 1826-1863

Marriage and Death Notices from Upper South Carolina Newspapers, 1843-1865

Marriage, Death, and Estate Notices from Georgetown, South Carolina Newspapers, 1791-1861

Marriages of Bute and Warren Counties, North Carolina, 1764-1868

Marriages of Granville County, North Carolina, 1753-1868

Marriages of Johnston County, North Carolina, 1762-1868

Marriages of Mecklenburg County, North Carolina, 1783-1868

Marriages of Orange County, North Carolina, 1779-1868

Marriages of Rowan County, North Carolina

Marriages of Rutherford County, North Carolina, 1779-1868

Marriages of Surry County, North Carolina, 1779-1868

Marriages of Wilkes County, North Carolina, 1778-1868

Mecklenburg County, North Carolina Abstracts of Early Wills, 1763-1790 (1749-1790)

Mecklenburg County, North Carolina Deed Abstracts, 1763-1779, Books 1-9

Memorialized Records of Lexington District, South Carolina, 1814-1825

Newberry County, South Carolina Deed Abstracts: Volume 1: Deed Books A-B, 1785-1794 (1751-1794)

Newberry County, South Carolina Deed Abstracts: Volume 2: Deed Books C, D-2, and D, 1794-1800 (1765-1800)

Newberry County, South Carolina Deed Abstracts: Volume 3: Deed Books E through H, 1800-1806 (1767-1806)

Newberry County, South Carolina Minutes of the County Court, 1785-1798

Ninety-Six District, South Carolina: Journal of the Court of Ordinary, Inventory Book, Will Book, 1781-1786
Brent Holcomb and Marguerite Clark.

North Carolina Land Grants in South Carolina

Orangeburgh District, South Carolina Estate Partitions from the Court of Equity, 1824-1837

Parish Registers of Prince George Winyah Church, Georgetown, South Carolina, 1815-1936

Passenger Arrivals at the Port of Charleston, 1820-1829

Petitions for Land from the South Carolina Council Journals Volume I: 1734/5-1748

Petitions for Land from the South Carolina Council Journals Volume II: 1748-1752

Petitions for Land from the South Carolina Council Journals Volume III: 1752-1753

Petitions for Land from the South Carolina Council Journals Volume IV: 1754-1756

Petitions for Land from the South Carolina Council Journals Volume V: 1757-1765

Record of Deaths in Columbia, South Carolina and Elsewhere as Recorded by John Glass, 1859-1877

South Carolina Deed Abstracts, 1773-1778, Books F-4 to X-5

South Carolina Deed Abstracts, 1776-1783, Books Y-4 to H-5

South Carolina Deed Abstracts, 1783-1788, Books I-5 to Z-5

South Carolina Marriages, 1688-1799

South Carolina Marriages, 1800-1820

South Carolina Naturalizations, 1783-1850

South Carolina's Confederate Pensioners in 1901

Spartanburg County, South Carolina Minutes of the County Court, 1785-1799

Spartanburg County, South Carolina Will Abstracts, 1787-1840

St. David's Parish, (Cheraw) South Carolina: Minutes of the Vestry, 1768-1832, and Parish Register, 1819-1924

Supplement to South Carolina Marriages, 1688-1820

The Bedenbaugh-Betenbaugh Family: Descendants of Johann Michael Bidenbach from Germany to South Carolina 1752

The South Carolina Magazine of Ancestral Research

Tryon County, North Carolina Minutes of the Court of Pleas and Quarter Sessions, 1769-1779

Union County, South Carolina Deed Abstracts, Volume I: Deed Books A-F, 1785-1800 (1752-1800)

Union County, South Carolina Deed Abstracts, Volume II: Deed Books G-K, 1800-1811 (1769-1811)

Union County, South Carolina Deed Abstracts, Volume III: 1811-1820 (1770-1820)

Union County, South Carolina Deed Abstracts, Volume IV: Deed Books Q-S, 1820-1828 (1779-1828)

Union County, South Carolina Minutes of the County Court, 1785-1799

Union County, South Carolina Will Abstracts, 1787-1849

Winton (Barnwell) County, South Carolina Minutes of County Court and Will Book 1, 1785-1791

York County, South Carolina Will Abstracts, 1787-1862

www.ingramcontent.com/pod-product-compliance
Lightning Source LLC
Chambersburg PA
CBHW080550170426
43195CB00016B/2738
* 9 7 8 0 7 8 8 4 1 6 8 9 7 *